33 -

5
ת/י2

VERTICAL

POETRY

by

ROBERTO JUARROZ

Translated from the Spanish by
W. S. MERWIN

NORTH POINT PRESS
San Francisco 1988

North Point Press
850 Talbot Avenue
Berkeley, CA
94706

Contents

Foreword

The poetry of Roberto Juarroz invites comparison with the work of a few of his near contemporaries, each of them radically different from him in temperament: Guillevic, for example, or Popa, or René Char, or Roseiwicz. Paradox is inseparable from the fabric of language and it recurs in the temptation to characterize things that are unique and original by resorting to comparisons. Setting the poetry of Juarroz in relatively appropriate company does indicate a few rather obvious things about it. A prevalent abstraction marks its drama and appears to direct the source and pace of its disclosures. The voice in the poems tends to be anonymous and disembodied, and the passion emerges as something intense but removed, distilled and timeless. Juarroz's poetry is farther from anecdote, and from the names and circumstances of what we sometimes call history, than that of the other poets I have named, or of almost any other poet I can think of. His literary ancestry and his kinships as a poet are not readily apparent, but it is consistent with everything revealed in his work that in an *œuvre* almost devoid of names and particular references he dedicated an important poem to the aphorist Antonio Porchia, an older man who was his close friend for years.

For the poetry of Juarroz has clear affinities with the aphoristic mode, from the crystallizations of whole cultures into proverbs, cryptic fragments, the apparently accidental aphorisms of the pre-Socratics, and the holograms of the *Tao Te Ching*, to the bell-notes of Blake and the resounding paragraphs of Nietzsche. Juarroz shares with this strain of utterance not only the combination of compression and distance but also the tone of conclusion. His poetry tends, like much aphoristic writing, to a cursive symmetry that appears at once to rise out of the subject itself and to become the immediate form of each evolving poem. In that sense, although it is neither metrical nor rhymed, the poetry of Juarroz is extremely formal, and the form is that of his own exploration and reflection among the abiding passions and the mysterious possibilities of existence. It is a kind of habit of motion in his language and thought, which becomes coherent and recognizable, at once impersonal and intimate. As we listen, it appears to be the natural representation of the cast of his own mind.

The form, manner, and tone of his poetry have been, indeed, remarkably consistent, distinct, and single-minded from the beginning—as consistent as the titles of his books themselves. The first of those (in 1958) was called *Vertical Poetry* (Poesía Vertical), the second (in 1963) *Second Vertical Poetry*, and so on, throughout the nine volumes so far. The individual poems do not have titles, but only numbers, as though they were instances, or pulses, of a single current. What Juarroz means, what he has meant from the outset by "vertical poetry," is something to be learned from the poems themselves, the roots and aspirations implicit in their finished forms. There is a salient clue in the three-line poem that stands at the beginning of the first volume as a kind of prelude to everything that is to follow:

> Going up is only
> a little shorter or a little
> longer than going down.

with its inevitable allusion to Fragment 108 of Heraclitus: "The way up and the way down are the same." The echo suggests a certain kinship to Heraclitus himself and his intransigent mode, and perhaps also to the ironic vein that surfaces in our time in the existentialists and their evocations of the "absurd." It suggests as well a shrugging-off of the traditional arrogations and restrictions of post-Aristotelian Western logic, and invokes with that gesture the vast undomesticated authority that is the source of poetry. It is a manifestation also of something too easily overlooked in these poems—and in a great deal of poetry: humor, of a wry and lurking kind, but humor nevertheless, which suggests an affinity between Juarroz and some contemporary Polish poets. The poem, for example, that goes:

> I'm awake.
> I'm asleep.
> I'm dreaming that I'm awake.
> I'm dreaming that I'm asleep.
> I'm dreaming that I'm dreaming.
>
> I'm dreaming that I'm dreaming
> that I'm awake.
> I'm dreaming that I'm dreaming
>
> that I'm asleep.
> I'm dreaming that I'm dreaming
> that I'm dreaming.
>
> I'm awake.

or the more somber

> Life draws a tree (p. 83)

or, in a late poem which returns to the image of the prelude,

> The roads leading upward (p. 155).

The paradox of movement and form, of change and finality, haunts many of the poems. In one of them, in his second volume, he says (p. 43)

> There has to be a point
> where the journeys of forgetting stop
> and the forms remember.

When asked to remember his own journeys, Juarroz says, in a letter of August 26, 1986:

> . . . I confess to you that I have never been very interested in my biography. For one thing, it did not seem to be of much importance, and for another it strikes me as an accident, a mixture of chance and destiny, which might be quite different without being any more valuable to anyone else, and which can be redeemed only in the direction of my own inner life, and as it is transfigured in my poems. Life is of immense importance to me as it is lived, but less so as it is remembered and still less in the descriptions of it. Of course it's more complicated than that, but I can't help having a certain allergy to my own biography . . .
>
> I was born in a small country town, on October 5, 1925. There I had a relatively happy childhood, with waves or presentiments of solitude and mystery. I was descended on both sides from Basques, but my parents were Argentine. My father was a railroad stationmaster and until I was nine or ten I lived in the ambience of the long-distance trains, which for me were filled with the spirit of travel and adventure.
>
> There were two other important elements in my childhood: nature (the earth, the pampa, the open countryside, the vast silence, a few trees, many birds, animals, rain, wind, skies without end, sea, and so on). And religion (the Catholic Church, the prayers, the books of devotion and piety, the converse with priests and monks, the religious school, and so on).
>
> I had an elder brother and an elder sister, many cousins; there were games and family feuds, and I knew sicknesses, affection, disillusions, a number of fantasies, and a certain inclination to be by myself, to solitary amusements. When I was about ten, my father was transferred, to be the stationmaster at a town on the outskirts of Buenos Aires: Adrogué. Borges lived there for a while, and wrote at some length about its tree-shaded streets, its parks full of secrets, its old mansions, its villa that was half ghost. I finished grade school and high school in Adrogué, and lived an adolescence interwoven with awakenings and more or less mystical feelings, fell in love a few times, knew the first great literary enthusiasms, the first poetic discoveries and the first poetic babblings of my own, writing as something more than an imitated gesture, the great nights of reading and solitude, of poetry and contemplation. I felt all that as the culmination, the summit of reality. And I was

marked by it once and for all. Several crucial meetings, the onset of great doubts, the rending of elemental desertions. My father died in my arms, of lung cancer, and I breathed death. I turned away from the church and its splendors, but I was tinged with something approaching mysticism, which appears and reappears in my poetry, which nowadays is my only religion, but in that non-confessional, primal, and open sense of which Novalis was speaking when he described poetry as the original religion of humanity.

There in Adrogué I came to know financial straits too, and I took my first job, at seventeen or eighteen, as a librarian (my "profession" from then on) at the Colegio Nacional. I formed a few close friendships, came to a better appreciation of the goodness of my mother, and the family egos; and then came the great discussions, the necessary partings, the return, each time more deeply, to poetry, the great renunciations for the sake of it (first fiancée and her fortune; my first studies at the university, which I gave up; my first local successes of an intellectual and cultural order; the outlines of a socio-literary life; and so on). There I burned many bridges and adopted in great part this fundamental solitude that has never forsaken me, in spite of all the activities, relations, and changes that life has brought me.

There too, contradictory though it seems, I entered on my first marriage, and had a daughter, when I was twenty-five or so. Then came my separation, and my first long travels—on land, to the south, Patagonia and its great un-peopled spaces, and by sea as an employee of a steamship company, a post from which I was subsequently expelled for political reasons. I came to know New York, several Latin American countries, the southern ports, and so on. Later I returned to my job as librarian, which I kept for some twenty years, not counting accidents and exiles that were more or less compulsory. I worked at that time four hours a day, in the morning, and devoted the rest of the time to reading, to poetry, and all the rest.

When I was thirty I decided to study, at the University of Buenos Aires, what had been my livelihood and would serve me as a means of subsistence: what is known as "Library Science." It was hard to make myself do it but I managed to graduate. It was at that time that I came to know Laura, became united to her, and she became my irreplaceable companion.

Then I was awarded a grant and went to Paris for a year. I discovered Europe, and set out on a real pilgrimage to the sources, which for several months Laura shared with me. When I came back, at the end of the grant, I was named to my first professorial post at the University, where I went on from stage to stage of a long teaching career, through innumerable changes, moves, indeed outrages, until I attained the position of full professor and head of my department.

I have always detested politics, and believe it to be—whatever its color—the greatest adversary of poetry. I have said so everywhere and under every government. And so I have paid for it: I was arbitrarily discharged three times, twice from the University and once earlier. Recently I submitted my-self in another competition and was given the post—for how long remains to be seen.

I have spent several years in forced exile from this country. In late 1977, when I was in Temperley, I underwent a serious crisis, a heart attack, which came in addition to other serious health problems that I already had.

Like many others, I have been through an infinity of things. I feel the unique richness of life and, as an unforgettable character of Bergman's said, 'I feel as though I were ten years old.' The rest, what really matters, you know. More than anything I love poetry, as the extreme creation of human kind. I feel more than ever an apprentice. I know that I have written something relatively different. I am not interested in literary success nor in being rich, nor in the socio-literary farce. I want something open and clear. I keep a few great admirations (Porchia, for example, and Rilke and Huidobro). I have always had a number of close friends; man matters deeply to me; I am a little startled by this growing recognition in recent years, and the voices that reach me from many directions; but I have a profound faith in something that I can only intimate in my poems, and I would like to live a little longer.

One other letter, this one from Julio Cortázar, written after the publication of *Second Vertical Poetry*, and published by Juarroz in the next volume, indicates how Juarroz is regarded by some of his contemporaries in Latin America:

Friend Juarroz: Forgive me for having taken so long to answer you, but I got back from Paris only a little while ago, after several months of working in Vienna. I've wanted to tell you for some time that the magazine (*Poesía* = *Poesía*) is precious to me because it allows me to hear, from so far away, the new young voices of Argentina. But I am writing you now for another, more urgent reason: I have just read *Second Vertical Poetry* and I am filled with wonder, without taking that step backward that we inevitably take when a poet has made us advance a bit closer to the great truth of this world, of the world. Your poems seem to me the loftiest and the deepest (the one by means of the other, of course) that have been written in Spanish in these years. I have had the feeling all the time that you manage to catch sight of what you are seeking with the same vision altogether devoid of impurities (verbal, dialectical, historical) that characterized, at the dawn of our world, the pre-Socratic poets, those whom the professors call *philosophers*: Parmenides, Thales, Anaxagoras, Heraclitus. You have only to look around you to have every prosaic appearance collapse in fragments in the presence of that total empowerment of being brought about by poetry. I have read aloud the poems that I understand best (others elude me or call for some interpretation, which may be a consolation for not grasping them the first time round) and each time I felt again a prodigious wonder, a sense of being caught up, of revelation. I have always loved a poetry that proceeds by inversion of signs: the use of absence in Mallarmé, certain "anti-essences" of Macedonio; the silences in the music of Webern. But you are master, to an incredible degree, of those inversions which in other hands end up as mere wordplay. And so that "look which sees and the look which does not see," once "twisted into a single thread," are something prodigiously rich, are "invention of being." It is a long time since I have read poems that have undone me as yours have, and this is said on the run, and without re-reading, because in the end one becomes silly, and shy of so many resounding words. But I know that you will believe me and that we are friends, and an embrace to you, *Julio Cortázar*

The name of the little town in which Juarroz was born in 1925 is Coronel Dorrego, Prov. de Buenos Aires.

As noted, his first book, *Vertical Poetry*, was published in 1958, in Buenos Aires. The next, *Second Vertical Poetry*, followed in 1963. The third, with Cortázar's letter as a prologue, in 1965. The fourth in 1969; fifth in 1974; sixth, published in Caracas, in 1976, in a volume of collected poetry from 1958 to 1975. *Seventh Vertical Poetry* was published in Buenos Aires in 1982, and the eighth in 1984. He has been published in French, in translations by Roger Caillois, Fernand Verhesen, and Roger Munier, in editions from 1962 to the present, and groups of poems have been translated and published in German, Italian, Portuguese, Greek, Danish, Dutch, Rumanian, Hindi, Arabic, and several other languages. In 1980 he published a series of dialogues with Guillermo Boido, *Poesía y Creación*. His ninth volume of *Vertical Poetry* is scheduled for publication in Mexico City (Edición Papeles Privados) and a second edition of his collected poems is scheduled for publication in Caracas.

From 1958 to 1965 he was the editor of the magazine *Poesía = Poesía*, and he has written as a literary critic and as a film critic, and has also translated a number of volumes. His writing has been the subject of many critical essays in Spanish and French.

In 1977 he was awarded the Gran Premio de Honor de la Fundacíon Argentina para la Poesía, and in 1984 the Premio Esteban Echeverría, given at the annual meeting of the Asociación Gente de Letras de Buenos Aires. In 1980 he was invited to Paris for the publication of a large French edition of his poetry published by Fayard, and other invitations of the same kind followed, in 1981 to Venezuela, in 1982 to Madrid, in 1983 to Santo Domingo, and in 1984, as part of an "homage to Octavio Paz" (who had written on Juarroz's poetry) to Mexico City. In 1984 he was elected a member of the Academia Argentina de Letras.

He has, besides, had a full career as a bibliographer and professor, has directed the Curso Audiovisual de Bibliotecnología para América Latina, and has published papers and attended congresses in the field of his "profession," in cities from Buenos Aires to Copenhagen. He is an honorary member of the faculties of the University of Costa Rica, of Antioquia in Colombia, and of the Universidad Mayor de San Andres in La Paz, Bolivia. In July, 1985, as part of a reorganization of the university, he was made a full professor at the University of Buenos Aires.

W. S. Merwin
Ha'iku, Hawaii

First
Vertical
Poetry

||||

[1958]

Going up is only
a little shorter or a little
longer than going down

Ir hacia arriba no es nada más
que un poco más corto o un poco
más largo que ir hacia abajo.

A net of looking
holds the world together,
keeps it from falling.
And although I don't know how it is with the blind,
my eyes go to rest on a back
that may be a god's.
Nevertheless
they look for another net, another thread
that goes along closing eyes with a borrowed garment
and takes down a rain that now has no earth and no sky.
My eyes look for what
makes us take off our shoes
to see if there is something holding us up from beneath
or invent a bird
to see whether the air exists
or create a world
to find out whether there's a god
or put our hat on
to prove that we exist.

———————————————————————————————————⊣1

Una red de mirada
mantiene unido al mundo,
no lo deja caerse.
Y aunque yo no sepa qúe pasa con los ciegos,
mis ojos van a apoyarse en una espalda
que puede ser de dios.
Sin embargo,
ellos buscan otra red, otro hilo,
que anda cerrando ojos con un traje prestado
y descuelga una lluvia ya sin suelo ni cielo.
Mis ojos buscan eso
que nos hace sacarnos los zapatos
para ver si hay algo más sosteniéndonos debajo
o inventar un pájaro
para averiguar si existe el aire
o crear un mundo
para saber si hay dios
o ponernos el sombrero
para comprobar que existimos.

Sometimes death grazes our hair,
rumples it
and does not enter.

Some great thought perhaps giving it pause?
Or can it be that we are thinking
something greater than thought itself?

2 |————————————————————————|

La muerte nos roza a veces los cabellos,
nos despeina
y no entra.

¿La detendrá quizás algún gran pensamiento?
¿O acaso pensamos
algo mayor que el pensamiento mismo?

Being begins between my human hands.
Being,
all the hands,
any word that is said in the world,
the labor of your death,
God, who does not labor.

But not being also begins between my human hands.
Not being,
all the hands,
the word that is said outside the world,
the vacation of your death,
God's weariness,
the mother who will never have a son,
my not dying yesterday.

But my human hands—where do they begin?

3

El ser empieza entre mis manos de hombre.
El ser,
todas las manos,
cualquier palabra que se diga en el mundo,
el trabajo de tu muerte,
Dios, que no trabaja.

Pero el no ser también empieza entre mis manos de hombre.
El no ser,
todas las manos,
la palabra que se dice afuera del mundo,
las vacaciones de tu muerte,
la fatiga de Dios,
la madre que nunca tendrá hijo,
mi no morir ayer.

Pero mis manos de hombre ¿dónde empiezan?

The bottom of things is neither life nor death.
My proof is
the air that goes barefoot in the birds,
a roof of absences that makes room for the silence,
and this look of mine that turns around at the bottom
as everything turns around at the end.

And my further proof is
my childhood that was bread before wheat,
my childhood that knew
that there were smokes that descend,
voices that nobody uses for talking,
roles in which a man does not move.

The bottom of things is neither life nor death.
The bottom is something else
that sometimes comes out on top.

4 |———————————————————————————————————|

El fondo de las cosas no es la vida o la muerte.
Me lo prueban
el aire que se descalza en los pájaros,
un tejado de ausencias que acomoda el silencio
y esta mirada mía que se da vuelta en el fondo,
como todas las cosas se dan vuelta cuando acaban.

Y también me lo prueba
mi niñez que era pan anterior a la harina,
mi niñez que sabía
que hay humos que descienden,
voces con las que nadie habla,
papeles donde el hombre está inmóvil.

El fondo de las cosas no es la muerte o la vida.
El fondo es otra cosa
que alguna vez sale a la orilla.

I don't want to get God mixed up with God.

That's why I don't wear a hat now,
I look for eyes in peoples' eyes,
and I ask myself what it is that won't let us wake,
while I'm here, in parentheses,
and thinking that everything may be a parenthesis.
While I finger this death with its train schedule
and trace lines around my hands.
Because that may be the whole game:
tracing lines around your hands
or the place of the hands.
Tracing lines around yourself inside parentheses,
not outside.

I don't want to get god mixed up with god.

No quiero confundir a Dios con Dios.

Por eso ya no uso sombrero,
busco ojos en los ojos de la gente
y me pregunto qué es lo que no nos deja despertar,
mientras estoy aquí, entre paréntesis,
y sospecho que todo es un paréntesis.
Mientras manoseo esta muerte con horario de trenes
y me calco las manos.
Porque tal ves todo el juego sea ése:
calcarse uno las manos
o el lugar de las manos.
Calcarse entre paréntesis,
no afuera.

No quiero confundir a dios con dios.

We will all die,
everyone that we've looked at, facing or sideways,
touched or conversed with or forgotten.
We will die one by one, frankly,
of this great impossible that is death.
The black color of my dog will die too,
the white color of your voice,
the hollow color of this day.
And meanwhile
we'll do one thing or another,
no longer so frankly,
but what difference will it make what we do?
Maybe it would be all the same
if my dog were white,
if your voice were black,
or if this day dyed us god-color.
Or maybe it wouldn't be the same,
and there the question has scarcely begun.

6 |————————————————————————

Nos moriremos todos,
todos cuantos nos hemos mirado, de frente o de reojo,
tocado o conversado u olvidado.
Nos moriremos uno a uno, francamente,
de este gran imposible que es la muerte.
También se morirá el color negro de mi perro,
el color blanco de tu voz,
el color hueco de este día.
Y mientras tanto
haremos una cosa u otra cosa,
ya no tan francamente,
¿pero qué importa lo que haremos?
Tal vez diera lo mismo
que mi perro tuviese el color blanco,
que tu voz fuera negra
o que este día nos tiñese de dios.
O tal vez no dé lo mismo
y ahí recién empiece la cuestión.

There are points of silence circling the heart.
They are itself, but facing it,
reclining on its multiple days,
not undone at its death, but on terms with her.

It is not a writing of silence looking for an eye,
nor a God safe outside himself,
nor a cowardly rain,
nor a dog tormented by his own barking.

The heart is a silent hand
with its fingers facing it.
It imitates their throbbing
but they won't be tempted.

—————————————————————————————|7

Hay puntos de silencio rodeando al corazón.
Son él mismo, pero enfrente,
recostado en sus múltiples fechas,
no deshecho en su muerte, pero en tratos con ella.

No es una escritura de silencio en busca de ojo,
ni un Dios asegurado afuera de sí mismo,
ni una lluvia cobarde,
ni un perro perseguido por su propio ladrido.

El corazón es una mano silenciosa
cuyos dedos están enfrente suyo.
El los imita a latidos,
pero ellos no se dejan seducir.

I don't know whether everything is god.
I don't know whether anything is god.
But every word names god:
shoe, strike, heart, collective.

And what's more
burnt-down collective,
old shoe,
general strike,
heart beside ruins.
And furthermore
collective with no one there,
shoe with no sole,
general strike of the dead,
heart in the ruins of the air.
And still furthermore
motionless collective for gods,
show for walking through the words,
strike of the dead in worn-out clothes,
heart with the blood of the ruins.

8 ├────────────────────────────────

No sé si todo es dios.
No sé si algo es dios.
Pero toda palabra nombra a dios:
zapato, huelga, corazón, colectivo.

Y más
colectivo incendiado,
zapato viejo,
huelga general,
corazón junto a ruinas.
Y más todavía
colectivo sin hombre,
zapato sin suela,
huelga general de los muertos,
corazón en las ruinas del aire.
Y más todavía
inmóvil colectivo para dioses,
zapato para andar por las palabras,
huelga de los muertos con la ropa gastada,
corazón con la sangre de las ruinas.

And furthermore.
But never mind.
I've stopped praying.
I'm going looking for the back of god.

Y más.
Pero no importa.
Ya he dejado de orar.
Voy a buscar ahora las espaldas de dios.

I think that at this moment
maybe nobody in the universe is thinking about me,
I'm the only one who's thinking me,
and if I were to die now
nobody, not even I, would think me.

And this is where the abyss begins,
as when I go to sleep.
I'm my own support and I take it away from me.
I help to curtain everything with absence.

That may be why
when you think of someone
it's like saving them.

9 |————————————————————————

Pienso que en este momento
tal vez nadie en el universo piensa en mí,
que sólo yo me pienso,
y si ahora muriese,
nadie, ni yo, me pensaría.

Y aquí empieza el abismo,
como cuando me duermo.
Soy mi propio sostén y me lo quito.
Contribuyo a tapizar de ausencia todo.

Tal vez sea por esto
que pensar en un hombre
se parece a salvarlo.

I found a man writing on his bones,
and I who have never seen a God
know that that man looks like a God.

There was something in his expression
that was the same as the norm or the odor of the suicide,
an abyss or a silence
that divides the universe into two precise and nocturnal parts.

He was writing on his bones
as on the sand of a beach burrowed into from above
and with the integrity of an eye
that could keep its thought inside itself.

But I could not look over his shoulder
to see what he was writing
because he was writing on his shoulder too.

———————————————————————————————————— 10

Hallé un hombre escribiendo en sus huesos
y yo, que nunca he visto un Dios,
sé que ese hombre se parece a un Dios.

Había en su gesto algo
equivalente a la norma o el olor del suicida,
un abismo o un silencio
que divide al universo en dos partes exactas y nocturnas.

Escribía en sus huesos
como en la arena de una playa horadada desde arriba
y con la integridad de un ojo
que encerrara en sí mismo también al pensamiento.

Pero no pude mirar sobre su hombro
para ver qué escribía,
porque también en su hombro escribía.

A great living rain
is striking me here on the forehead
and asking me to come in, I don't know where.

A great dead rain
is striking me here on the forehead
and asking me to go out, I don't know where.

And I'm waiting for another rain,
the third,
the one that hits me here on the forehead
just to be with me.

And I won't even have to ask it
whether it's alive or dead.

11

Una gran lluvia viva
me pega aquí en la frente
y me pide que entre a no sé dónde.

Una gran lluvia muerta
me pega aquí en la frente
y me pide que salga a no sé dónde.

Y yo espero otra lluvia,
la tercera,
la que me pegue aquí en la frente
sencillamente para estar conmigo.

Y ni siquiera habré de preguntarle
si ella está viva o muerta.

I have mistaken almost everything
except the center.

But sometimes the center goes out
heavily, to put the hands to flight,
eternity of course and the hands,
with the vulgarity of any God.

Then, and no doubt about it,
I feel I want to leave the center out there
and remain inside alone and simple
like any man.

—————————————————————————————|12

He equivocado todo o casi todo,
menos el centro.

Pero el centro a veces se va afuera,
a derrotar torpemente a las manos,
la eternidad por supuesto y las manos,
con la vulgaridad de un Dios cualquiera.

Entonces, y sin equivocarme,
siento ganas de dejar el centro afuera
y quedarme yo solo y simple adentro,
como un hombre cualquiera.

Sometimes my hands wake me up.
They're making or taking apart something without me
while I'm asleep,
something terribly human,
concrete like the back or the pocket of a man.

I hear them from inside my sleep,
working out there,
but when I open my eyes they're still.
Just the same
I've thought that maybe I'm a man
because of what they do
with their appearance and not mine,
with their God and not mine,
with their death, if they die too.

13

A veces mis manos me despiertan.
Ellas hacen o deshacen algo sin mí,
mientras yo duermo,
algo terriblemente humano,
concreto como la espalda o el bolsillo de un hombre.

Las oigo desde el sueño
en su labor afuera,
pero al abrir los ojos ya están quietas.
Sin embargo,
he pensado que tal vez yo sea hombre
por eso que ellas hacen
con su gesto y no el mío,
con su Dios y no el mío,
con su muerte, si también ellas mueren.

I don't know how to make a man.
Maybe my hands make one while I'm asleep
and when it's finished
they wake me up completely
and show it to me.

Y no sé hacer un hombre.
Tal vez lo hagan mis manos mientras duermo
y cuando esté acabado
me despierten del todo
y me lo muestren.

There are clothes that last longer than love.
There are clothes that start out from death
and go around the world
and around two worlds.

There are clothes that instead of wearing out
get newer all the time.

There are clothes just for taking off.

There are vertical clothes.

The fall of man
stands them on their feet.

Hay trajes que duran más que el amor.
Hay trajes que comienzan con la muerte
y dan la vuelta al mundo
y a dos mundos.

Hay trajes que en lugar de gastarse
se vuelvan cada vez más nuevos.

Hay trajes para desvestirse.

Hay trajes verticales.

La caída del hombre
los pone de pie.

The glance is a lovely pretext of the eye's
and death also is a pretext
though not so lovely.
The thorns maintain our blood,
and there is a new sex of people
that has discovered God.

We can wipe out the glances
and bury death
even though it is filling the world
like a vast smoke in flower.
We can hammer all the thorns into ourselves
and even draw a perfect likeness of God.

But we can't join up the eye with death
nor the thorn with god.

—————————————————————— 15

La mirada es un hermoso pretexto del ojo
y la muerte también es un pretexto,
aunque no tan hermoso.
Las espinas nos sostienen la sangre
y hay un nuevo sexo de gente
que ha descubierto a Dios.

A las miradas podemos borrarlas
y a la muerte enterrarla,
aunque esté llenando el mundo
como un gran humo en flor.
Podemos clavarnos todas las espinas
y hasta dibujar perfectamente a Dios.

Pero no podemos juntar el ojo con la muerte,
ni la espina con dios.

By now death won't face the mirrors.
Afraid of erasing or breaking them.
And much more afraid
of being erased or of breaking.

Just the same
there's always one mirror left watching itself in death
as though death were simply
a mirror of mirrors,
one mirror facing another
with nothing now in between.

16 ──────────────────────────────────

La muerte ya no enfrenta a los espejos.
Tiene miedo de borrarlos o romperlos.
Y más, mucho más miedo tiene
de borrarse o de romperse.

Sin embargo,
siempre queda un espejo que se mira en la muerte,
como si ella fuera simplemente
un espejo de espejos,
un espejo que se enfrenta con otro,
ya sin nada en el medio.

Yes, there is a back of things.

But there is also a beyond the back of things,
a place made of faces turned backwards.

And in that place there are footfalls,
footfalls or at least the waiting for footfalls,
the reading of a blind man who no longer needs braille
and reads from the smoothness,
or maybe a deaf man's reading
from a dead man's lips.

Yes, there is a back of things.

But it is the place where the other side begins,
symmetrical with this one,
maybe this one repeated,
maybe this one and its double,
maybe this one.

———|17

Sí, hay un fondo.

Pero hay también un más allá del fondo,
un lugar hecho con caras al revés.

Y allí hay pisadas,
pisadas o por lo menos su anticipo,
lectura de ciego que ya no necesita puntos
y lee en lo liso
o tal vez lectura de sordo
en los labios de un muerto.

Sí, hay un fondo.

Pero es el lugar donde empieza el otro lado,
simétrico de éste,
tal vez éste repetido,
tal vez éste y su doble,
tal vez éste.

Man,
puppet of night,
stabs voids.

But one day
a void in a rage stabs him back.

After that there is nothing
but a dagger in the void.

18 |————————————————————————

El hombre,
maniquí de la noche,
apuñala vacíos.

Pero un día,
un vacío le devuelve feroz la puñalada.

Y sólo queda entonces
un puñal en la nada.

There are times when I can't move.

I feel roots of mine everywhere,
as though all things were born of me
or as though I were born of all things.

All I can do then is to stay still
with eyes open like two faces at the moment of birth,
with a small amount of love in one hand
and something cold in the other.

And all I can give someone passing by me
is that motionless absence
that has roots in him too.

A veces ya no puedo moverme.

Hallo raíces mías en todas partes,
como si todas las cosas nacieran de mí
o como si yo naciera de todas las cosas.

Sólo puedo entonces quedarme quieto,
con los ojos abiertos como dos rostros a punto de nacer,
con un poco de amor en una mano
y algo de frío en la otra.

Y a quien pasa a mi lado
tan sólo puedo darle esa ausencia inmóvil
con la raíz también en él.

Only a human has weight on the earth,
a history of deaths
grown between the legs.

And does not know it,
yet knows everything,
since only a human
has the mouth open,
the heart lost between the teeth,
and the head more naked than God.

All the weight is in the connections,
in the void of his mouth,
the little line of his skin,
his shape in the mirror,
the sail they dress him in,
and the well they dig for him
any day.

20

Sólo el hombre tiene peso en la tierra.
una historia de muertes
crecida entre las piernas.

El no lo sabe,
pero todo lo sabe,
pues solamente el hombre
tiene la boca abierta,
el corazón perdido entre los dientes
y desnuda más que Dios la cabeza.

Todo el peso está en sus comisuras,
en el vacío de su boca,
la rayita de su piel,
su figura en el espejo,
la vela que le prenden
y el pozo que le hacen
cualquier día.

There may be another place
where all the rest has weight,
the things and the angels.

But a human
wouldn't have any weight there:
nobody would be there.

Tal vez haya otro sitio
en donde todo lo otro pese,
las cosas y los ángeles.

Pero el hombre
allí no tendrá peso,
allí no será nadie.

Our hands deceive us too.

The truth is we don't have any hands
which is why we lose everything,
stone or life.

We don't have any hands.

And the ambiguous antecedents of God
have no way of hiding
this floating stump in which we flow out,
in which maybe everything flows out.

21 ├──

Las manos también nos engañan.

La verdad es que no tenemos manos
y por eso lo perdemos todo,
una piedra o la vida.

No tenemos manos.

Y los ambiguos antecedentes de Dios
no alcanzan de ninguna manera
para tapar este muñón flotante en el cual desembocamos
y en el cual tal vez todo desemboque.

It shouldn't be possible
to sleep without keeping beside you
a voice to wake yourself up with.

It shouldn't be possible
to sleep without keeping beside you
your own voice to wake yourself up with.

It shouldn't be possible
to sleep without waking
just at the moment when sleep
meets those open eyes
that don't need sleep any more.

———————————————————————————— 22

No debiera ser posible
dormirse sin tener cerca
una voz para poderse despertar.

No debiera ser posible
dormirse sin tener cerca
la propia voz para poderse despertar.

No debiera ser posible
dormirse sin despertar
en el momento justo en que el sueño se encuentra
con esos ojos abiertos
que ya no necesitan dormir más.

Something hurts us without us
while our hands turn like ghosts
and our back splashes our voice.

Something hurts us like a bone
beyond the other bones,
together with eyes neither blind nor seeing,
in the word that kills our words
even to the shadow they leave us.

Along with all the pain something hurts us
like a star forced to invent another heaven for itself.

And by now it hurts us without our being,
but in the center and forever,
though eternity may not exist
and we may be what is left over.

23 ────────────────────────────────

Algo nos duele sin nosotros,
mientras las manos giran como duendes
y la espalda nos salpica la voz.

Algo nos duele como un hueso
que estuviera más allá de los huesos,
junto a unos ojos sin ceguera ni mirada,
en la palabra que nos mata las palabras
y hasta la sombra que ellas dejan.

Junto a todo el dolor algo nos duele,
como una estrella obligada a inventarse otro cielo.

Y ya nos duele sin nuestro propio ser,
pero en el centro y para siempre,
aunque la eternidad no exista
y aunque estemos de más.

A man spells out his weariness.
All at once as he spells
he meets some strange capital letters,
unexpectedly alone,
unexpectedly tall.
They weigh more on the tongue.
They weigh more but they get away
faster and he can hardly
pronounce them.
His heart crowds into the roads
where death is exploding.
And he meets, as he goes on spelling,
more and more strange capital letters.
And a great fear chokes him
of finding a word
written all in capitals
and not being able to pronounce it.

———————————————————————————————— ⊣ **24**

El hombre deletrea su cansancio.
Deletrea y de pronto
encuentra unas mayúsculas extrañas,
inesperadamente solas,
inesperadamente altas.
Pesan más en la lengua.
Pesan más pero escapan
con más prisa y apenas
si puede pronunciarlas.
Su corazón se agolpa en los caminos
donde la muerte estalla.
Y encuentra, mientras sigue deletreando,
cada vez más mayúsculas extrañas.
Y un gran temor le ahoga:
hallar una palabra
escrita solamente con mayúsculas
y no poder entonces pronunciarla.

There will come a day
when we won't need to push on the panes for them to fall
nor hammer the nails for them to hold
nor walk on the stones to keep them quiet
nor drink the faces of women for them to smile.

It will be the beginning of the great union.
Even God will learn how to talk,
and the air and the light
will enter their cave of shy eternities.

Then there will be no more difference between your eyes and
        your belly
nor between my words and my mouth.
The stones will be like your breasts
and I will make my verses with my hands
so that nobody can be mistaken.

25 ├──┤

Llegará un día
en el cual no habrá que empujar los vidrios para que caigan,
ni martillar los clavos para que sostengan,
ni pisar las piedras para que se callen,
ni beber el rostro de las mujeres para que sonrían.

Empezará la gran unión.
Hasta Dios aprenderá a hablar
y el aire y la luz
entrarán en su cueva de miedosas eternidades.

Entonces ya no habrá diferencia entre tus ojos y tu vientre,
ni entre mis palabras y mi voz.
Las piedras serán como tus senos
y yo haré mis versos con las manos,
para que nadie pueda ya confundirse.

My face is looking at me out of the dust.

I don't know out of what I'm looking at it,
but there is growing between us like a ruined curtain
the naked distance,
the distance nobody will occupy.

—————————————————————————————————| 26

Mi rostro me está mirando desde el polvo.

Yo no sé desde dónde lo miro,
pero entre ambos crece como un telón en ruinas
la distancia desnuda,
la distancia que nadie ocupará.

Where is the heart I am calling?
Heart become eyelid
of an eye on its way to where I am.
The eye is not here yet and already I can see.
Before there is a heart I am made of beating.
I am calling in an open doorway.
I am calling from inside.

27 ├──────────────────────────────────────┤

¿Dónde está el corazón adonde llamo?
Corazón hecho párpado
de un ojo que ya viene hacia mi sitio.
El ojo aún no ha llegado y yo ya veo.
Antes del corazón soy de latidos.
Estoy llamando en una puerta abierta.
Estoy llamando desde adentro mismo.

With my mouth in one hand
and my death in the other
I question the silence.
I draw marks on it,
I demand guarantees for the shout,
I calculate its dose of reply.

Something like a large sad animal
comes then to strip itself naked in my voice
but discovers that it was naked already.

Meanwhile,
one of my hands has been left empty.
But I will never know which.

28

Con la boca en una mano
y la muerte en la otra,
le hago cuestiones al silencio.
Le dibujo lunares,
le exijo garantías para el grito,
le calculo su dosis de respuesta.

Algo así como un gran animal triste
viene entonces a desnudarse en mi voz,
pero encuentra que ya estaba desnudo.

Mientras tanto,
una de mis dos manos se ha quedado vacía.
Y yo nunca sabré cuál de las dos.

I set my eyes backward
as at one time I set god forward
or the thoughtful touch with which I have loved.

And as at one time I set nothing
either forward or backward,
I turned my shadow
or the shadow, it may be, of something I don't find.

I set my eyes backward
and I die in back of me,
I die of no god and of no anybody.

May it not be that death
is a pure going backwards,
a going backwards with nobody?

29

Pongo los ojos hacia atrás,
como alguna vez puse a dios hacia adelante
o el tacto pensativo con que he amado.

Y como alguna vez no puse nada,
ni adelante ni atrás,
puse mi sombra
o quizá la de algo que no encuentro.

Pongo los ojos hacia atrás
y me muero atrás mío,
me muero de no dios y de no alguien.

¿Será la muerto acaso
un puro ir hacia atrás,
un irse atrás sin nadie?

Second

Vertical

Poetry

||||

[1963]

Ancient cries
still floating between things, like algae of sound,
catch in the aerial shores of my thought.
Then the centuries dissolve like crystals of oblivion
and I am again the first man
working his stitch through the foam
groping for footing among the bitter shuttles
that are weaving the mass of night.

Enough for one hair to touch bottom.

—— ⊣1

Antiguos gritos
que aún flotan como algas de sonido entre las cosas
se enredan en las costas de aire de mi pensamiento.
Los siglos se deshacen entonces como granulaciones de olvido
y soy de nuevo el primer hombre
trabajando su punto entre la espuma,
tratando de hacer pie entre las agrias lanzaderas
con que se teje el bulto de la noche.

Basta que un cabello toque el fondo.

A leap out of one's own hands,
turning into one's own toboggan,
inventing it as a dead bird would invent the air
if it started to fly again.
Not to wait for the blind trot of the fall.
To create it like a horizon
or maybe the credulous pasture of an invisible animal,
knowing that below is anywhere,
even the ancient site where a man with no company,
not even himself for company,
invented love.

A leap toward one's own hands.

2 ⊢───

Un salto desde las propias manos,
invirtiéndose uno mismo en su propio tobogán,
inventándolo como un pájaro muerto inventaría el aire
si volviese a su vuelo.
No esperar el trote ciego de la caída.
Crearla como si fuera un horizonte
o quizá el pasto crédulo de un animal invisible,
sabiendo que abajo es cualquier parte,
hasta el antiguo sitio donde un hombre sin nadie,
hasta sin él,
inventó el amor.

Un salto hacia las propias manos.

What matters is not to tie up the loose ends
but to feel the terminal experience of their tips.
The tips that we feel
melt into us
until they become only one.

And this is what matters
though nobody feels that tip any more
and though it turns us into the loosest end of all.

—————————————————————————————————————— 3

Lo que importa no es unir los cabos sueltos
sino sentir la experiencia terminal de sus extremos.
Los extremos que sentimos
se funden en nosotros
hasta convertirse en uno solo.

Y es eso lo que importa,
aunque a ese extremo ya no lo sienta nadie
y aunque él nos convierta en el cabo más suelto.

A transparent pulse
is moving a hand broken
with too much testing
of the formula of man.
A stalactite through which no drop ever flowed
presides over the reconstruction of the hand.
But then the hand turns
breaking for the last time,
toward its transparent pulse,
and finds, without trying,
the formula it was looking for.
If all transparence were a pulse
and all the rest were a hand
the formula of man would not be needed.

4 |————————————————————————————

Un pulso transparente
mueve una mano rota
por haber ensayado demasiado
la fórmula del hombre.
Una estalactita que no fue nunca gotera
planea la reconstrucción de la mano.
Pero ésta se vuelve entonces
por su última ruptura
hacia su pulso transparente
y en él encuentra sin ensayo
la fórmula que buscaba.
Si toda la transparencia fuera un pulso
y todo lo demás una mano,
la fórmula del hombre sobraría.

Only a few looks pass through the eyes
and there are others that don't pass through anywhere.
The earth, for example, looks..   .
Sometimes there is a well,
sometimes a sting in the wind,
sometimes a line along the water.
But sometimes nothing,
only the pure look of the earth,
the look in which we are beating.

———————————————————————————— 5

Sólo algunas miradas pasan por los ojos
y hay otras que no pasan por ninguna parte.
La tierra, por ejemplo, mira.
A veces hay un pozo,
a veces un excozor en el viento,
a veces una línea junto al agua.
Pero a veces no hay nada,
salvo la mirada pura de la tierra,
la mirada en que latimos.

The center isn't a point.
If it were, it would be easier to locate.
It's not even the reduction of a point to its infinity.

The center is an absence,
of a point, of infinity, even of absence,
and it can be located only by absence.

Look at me after you've gone
even though it's only a moment since I was there.
Now the center has taught me not to be here
but later this is where the center will be.

6 ⊢──

El centro no es un punto.
Si lo fuera, resultaría fácil acertarlo.
No es ni siquiera la reduccíon de un punto a su infinito.

El centro es una ausencia,
de punto, de infinito y aun de ausencia
y sólo se acierta con ausencia.

Mírame después que te hayas ido,
aunque yo esté recién cuando me vaya.
Ahora el centro me ha enseñado a no estar,
pero más tarde el centro estará aquí.

The stone is a clenched lap
where the bird's open maneuver is in peril,
but also it is an open memory
where the bird's clenched fist
plummets like an unexpected threat.

There has to be a point
where the journeys of forgetting stop
and the forms remember.

7

La piedra es un regazo crispado
donde corre peligro la maniobra abierta del pájaro,
pero es también una memoria abierta
donde el cerrado puño del pájaro
se desploma como una imprevista amenaza.

Tiene que haber un punto
donde cesen los turnos del olvido
y las formas recuerden.

Death is another way of looking.
The moon of the dead is older
and no longer makes tides.

And your own is another way of looking.
The moon of life was younger
and herself was the tide.

Between both moons,
before dying and after living,
we are a bone of looking
lying beside a sea that never begins.

8 |————————————————————

La muerte es otro modo de mirar.
La luna de los muertos es más vieja
y no fabrica ya mareas.

Tu modo de mirar también es otro.
La luna de la vida era más joven
y era ella misma la marea.

Entre ambas lunas,
antemuriendo o postviviendo,
somos un hueso de mirada
junto a un mar que no empieza.

The memories leap out of the eyes
like colors out of the cage of a light
that now admits only white.
They go to peck the cheeks
of certain things that wander lost through the world
and they return through the eyes again
to their forest of softness and other sides.

But there is one of them, a memory or tattoo,
that refuses to go back in through the eyes
and keeps circling like a mute exodus,
an eye itself, drifting toward nowhere,
a memory that has wiped out the past.

Won't the night, or maybe something deeper,
come and make another body for it, another secret forest
of miniature signals,
where without time the mirage of its loss
may be a still place between loving hands?

———————————————————————— 9

Los recuerdos saltan desde los ojos
como colores desde la jaula de una luz
que no admite más que el blanco,
se van a picotear las mejillas
de algunas cosas que andan perdidas por el mundo
y retornan, otra vez por los ojos,
a su selva de molicie y respaldos.

Pero hay uno, un recuerdo o tatuaje,
que no quiere pasar de nuevo por los ojos
y se queda dando vueltas como un éxodo mudo,
ojo él mismo, flotando hacia ninguna parte,
memoria que ha abolido el pasado.

¿No llegará la noche, o quizá algo más hondo,
a formarle otro cuerpo, otra privada selva
de minúscolos signos,
donde pueda, sin tiempo, su alucinante pérdida
ser un sitio y inmóvil entre manos amantes?

A belly dyed with foam
has gathered up the pieces of the house of the sea.
All that's missing is the deepest fish
of the first tenderness,
all that's missing is the glance that turned into hair
to understand the wind,
all that's missing is the form of the touch
of the first tree and the first light.

But there is a liquid sign that gathers together what is missing
like the line that draws the sea on the sea.

10 ⊢───⊢

Un vientre teñido de espuma
ha recogido los pedazos de la casa del mar.
Falta sólo el hondísimo pez de la primera ternura,
falta sólo la mirada que se volvió cabello
para entender al viento,
falta sólo la forma del contacto
del primer árbol con la primera luz.

Pero hay un líquido signo que une lo que falta,
como la línea que dibuja al mar en el mar.

An uncommitted gesture, a rapt expression,
moves something in the death of things,
among the hardened cries,
the smells of love that is over,
the women without shadows,
the shells of no one.
It is not a life full of holes
dripping and leaving stains,
it is not a forgotten name
trying to get loose from its object.
A gesture held up by nothing
has strayed into death,
more alone than things,
more alone than names
when they are left alone.

———————————————————————————————————| 11

Un gesto neutro, en ademán absorto,
mueve algo en la muerte de las cosas,
entre los gritos tiesos,
los olores a amor ya concluido,
las mujeres sin sombra,
las cáscaras de nadie.
No es la vida infiltrada
goteando sus manchones,
no es un nombre olvidado
que quiera despegarse de su objeto.
Un gesto sin sostén
se ha extraviado en la muerte,
más solo que las cosas,
más solo que los nombres
cuando se quedan solos.

Efficacy of the light,
efficacy of the cloud,
tricks of the efficacy of their absence.

The stick bell
is preparing a clang
louder than metal.
A bird is flying between two clouds
but there is another that flies
the whole time inside the cloud.

And there is yet another bird that raises
one wing outside and the other inside.

But now there is no more cloud.
No more light either.

12

Eficacia de la luz,
eficacia de la nube,
trampas de la eficacia de su ausencia.

La campana de palo
prepara un remolino
más sonoro que el metal.
Entre dos nubes vuela un pájaro,
pero hay otro que vuela
siempre adentro de la nube.

Y hay además un pájaro que lleva
un ala afuera y otra adentro.

Pero ya no hay más nube.
Ni tampoco más luz.

Unique each night,
the heart in the head, with no neck,
you travel the world in an echoing suit,
a flavor in garments of living waters,
crushing the sepia moon of the dead.

A walking which is a standing still,
without sunflower without tombs among the stars,
one foot root and the other cloud,
the eyes heart word thing,
the hands animals
in their forest of hands.

And among ravens, cripples and instruments,
your fist on the mountain of being only one,
awake even though you're sleeping,
explication of the word "man"
in the human place
where everything is in doubt.

———————————————————————————| 13

Nocturnamente único,
el corazón, sin cuello, en la cabeza,
caminas por el mundo con un traje sonoro,
sabor vestido de aguas vivas,
machacando la luna sepia de los muertos.

Andanza que es estar,
sin girasol ni tumbas por los astros,
un pie raíz y otro pie nube,
los ojos corazón palabra cosa,
las manos animales
en su selva de manos.

Y entre cuervos, lisiados e instrumentos,
tu puño en la montaña de ser uno,
despierto aunque te duermas,
aclaración de la palabra hombre
en el lugar humano
de la duda de todo.

At the sight of you, yes, I remember.
Never mind what or whom; I remember.
The skin is a solid wind
that communicates inward and outward
with the skin.

Al verte, sí, me acuerdo.
No importa de qué, de quién: me acuerdo.
La piel es un viento sólido
que comunica por adentro y afuera
con la piel.

The smoke of death
has turned the path into a moving stone.
What floor or twisting or frame
can give it rest now
or simply hold it up?
What skin can give it its wound
so that it can fulfill its impulse
or intention or gesture?

Or is the smoke of death
only a mirage,
the misleading refraction of a stone that never moves?

———————————————————————————————————┤14

El humo de la muerte
ha convertido el camino en una piedra que se mueve.
¿Qué piso o anfractuosidad o marco
podrá ahora darle descanso
o simplemente sostén?
¿Qué piel podrá darle su herida
para que se cumpla su impulso
o intención o gesto?

¿O el humo de la muerte
es tan sólo el espejismo,
la engañosa refracción de una piedra inmóvil?

Look first at the air and its black element that never stops,
look at the too-smooth backs of the things that death has been
    scraping,
look at the way the crooked view—man's view—is growing,
while the straight view is lying thrown out somewhere,
look at the way shores are passing rivers that are standing still,
and violent imitations of the heart are breaking spears,
look at the thunder of age and faces without end, which is biting
    the world,
look at the worn-out carillon of death
with its gnashing and biting itself to have something to bite,
and its lunatic passion for tombs and blots,
look at the nostrils that invent fragrances without hollows,
and at the bed that will arrive when we are not here
and at the snoring that is the seal of love.

Then and only then
sign and go through with it.

15

Véase primero el aire y su elemento negro que no cesa,
véase el lomo demasiado suave de las cosas que ha rozado la muerte,
véase cómo crece la mirada torcida, la mirada del hombre,
mientras la recta mirada de las cosas yace tirada en cualquier parte,
véase cómo hay orillas que pasan de ríos que no pasan
y violentas imitaciones del corazón rompiendo astas,
véase el trueno de vejez y gestos sin acabar que muerde al mundo,
véase el gastado carillón de la muerte,
su dentellada que por morder se muerde hasta a sí misma,
su lunático hipo de tumbas y borrones,
véase las narices que inventan fragancias sin vacíos
y el lecho que llegará cuando no estemos
y el ronquido que sella los amores.

Y tan sólo después
fírmese y cúmplase.

Sometimes the walls of sleep
lie down in the breast
and suddenly one sees
that sleep is a love that has lost its way,
a form of love that has remained unattached.
And it's no use trying to gather it in,
even by loving in sleep,
because love, when it passes,
becomes free of us
as the wind becomes free of the tree
or the night from the nearly abortive
gesture of its hours.
It becomes free of us and surrounds itself with walls.

—————————————————————————————| 16

Los muros del sueño
se recuestan a veces en el pecho
y súbitamente uno comprende
que el sueño es un amor extraviado,
una forma de amor que quedó suelta.
Y no vale tratar de recogerla,
ni aun amando dormidos,
pues el amor, cuando pasa,
se independiza de nosotros,
como el viento del árbol
o la noche del gesto casi absorto de sus horas.
Se independiza y se rodea de muros.

The disbelief of the stars
comes down to establish an unbalanced heretical light,
a new captivity of very small reflected pieces
that emigrate, nevertheless, from over there where there is
    nothing.
Choosing would be easy,
for this is the place where the tops spin
even though they know that they will stop,
and where another assymetrical light,
also a captive of what does not exist,
cannot find the heart to go away
and keeps splitting things,
taking them down like fruit
that has smuggled itself up into a tree.

Can one construct an embrace
out of two left arms,
or will its odd conclave remain left-handed?
Probably even one would be enough
if there were something to embrace.

17 ├───┤

La incredulidad de las estrellas
baja a fundar la asimetría de una herética luz,
un nuevo cautiverio de migajas reflejas
que emigran, sin embargo, de allí donde no hay nada.
La elección era fácil,
pues éste es el lugar donde los trompos giran
aun sabiendo que van a detenerse
y donde otra luz asimétrica,
tambíen cautiva de lo que no existe,
no se anima a partir
y va escindiendo las cosas,
desarmándolas como a frutos
que hubieran trepado de contrabando a un árbol.
¿Se podrá, con dos brazos izquierdos,
construir un abrazo,
o su cónclave impar seguirá zurdo?
Probablemente hasta uno solo bastaría
si hubiera algo que abrazar.

Words fall from the clouds.
They fall for the sake of falling,
not for anyone to pick them up.
They fall to recover strength
in the quietest tension.

Suddenly one of these words stops
as though suspended in the air.
Then I give it my own fall.

———————————————————————————————————— ⊣18

Caen palabras de las nubes
Caen para caer,
no para que alguien las recoja.
Caen para recuperarse
en la tensión más quieta.

De pronto,
una de esas palabras queda como suspendida en el aire.
Entonces, yo le doy mi caída.

Thinking robs us of looking.

Where then is the vision,
its thread of music without variations of sound,
its coincidence of eye and dream,
its space in which only motion finds space?
Where is the thought that robs nothing?

Though smaller than the others,
thinking is also an absence.
A forgetting, growing.
And also a staying alone
and opening the door in order to disappear.

19 ⊢─── ⊣

Pensar nos roba el mirar.

¿Dónde está entonces la visión,
su hebra de música sin variaciones de sonido,
su coincidencia de ojo y sueño,
su espacio donde sólo el pasar encuentra espacio?
¿Dónde está el pensamiento que no roba nada?

Aunque menor que otras,
pensar también es una ausencia.
Y un olvido que crece.
Y además quedarse solo
y abrir la puerta para desparecer.

A strand finer than thought,
a thread the caliber of nothing,
connects our eyes when we are not looking at each other.

When we look at each other
all the threads of the world connect us
but that one is missing;
it alone casts a shadow
in the most secret light of love.

After we've gone
maybe that thread will remain
connecting our empty places.

————————————————————————————————| 20

Una hebra más delgada que el pensamiento,
un hilo con calibre de nada,
une nuestros ojos cuando no nos miramos.

Cuando nos miramos
nos unen todos los hilos del mundo,
pero falta éste,
que sólo da sombra
a la luz más secreta del amor.

Después que nos vayamos,
quizá quede este hilo
uniendo nuestros sitios vacíos.

Each one goes however he can,
some with the breast ajar,
others with only one hand,
some with an identification in a pocket,
others with it in the soul,
some with the moon screwed into their blood,
and others without blood, or moon, or memories.

Each one goes, even though he can't,
some with love between their teeth,
others changing their skins,
some with life and death,
others with death and life,
some with their hand on their own shoulder,
others with it on somebody else's shoulder.

Each one goes because he's going,
some with someone up late between the eyebrows,
others whose paths never crossed anyone's,
some through the door that opens onto the road
or seems to,

21 ├──┤

Cada uno se va como puede,
unos con el pecho entreabierto,
otros con una sola mano,
unos con la cédula de identidad en el bolsillo,
otros en el alma,
unos con la luna atornillada en la sangre
y otros sin sangre, ni luna, ni recuerdos.

Cada uno se va aunque no pueda,
unos con el amor entre dientes,
otros cambiándose la piel,
unos con la vida y la muerte,
otros con la muerte y la vida,
unos con la mano en su hombro
y otros en el hombro de otro.

Cada uno se va porque se va,
unos con alguien trasnochado entre las cejas,
otros sin haberse cruzado con nadie,
unos por la puerta que da o parece dar sobre el camino,

others through the door that's drawn on the wall
or perhaps on the air,
some without having begun to live
and others without having begun to live.

But all of them go with their feet tied,
some by the path that they made,
others by the one they didn't make,
and all by the one that they will never make.

otros por una puerta dibujada en la pared o tal vez en el aire,
unos sin haber empezado a vivir
y otros sin haber empezado a vivir.

Pero todos se van con los pies atados,
unos por el camino que hicieron,
otros por el que no hicieron
y todos por el que nunca harán.

The last light always welds itself to the hand.
It's a fruit,
a body already complete.
After that
if a further return were possible
the whole body would see.
The light of the water is water,
the light of the shadow is the shadow,
and the light of one foot is the other foot.

22 |————————————————————————————————————|

La última luz se suelda siempre a la mano.
Es un fruto,
un cuerpo ya completo.
Si despueś de ella
fuera posible aún otro regreso,
todo el cuerpo vería.
La luz del agua es el agua,
la de la sombra, la sombra,
y la de un pie, el otro pie.

After half a life or maybe all of it
few things survive:
the place where the parallels tremble,
the night in which a dead love comes back to life,
an instance which is neither light, shadow, nor the shades
    between,
a place which is not the all minus the others,
certain introductions outwards.

Shapes of loyalties unknown to us—
only in them is it possible
to put off for a little while the impossibility of everything.

| 23

Después de media vida o quizá toda,
pocas cosas resisten:
el lugar donde las paralelas tiemblan,
la noche en que un amor muerto vuelve a estar vivo,
una instancia que no es la luz, la sombra ni sus gradaciones intermedias,
un sitio que no es el todo menos los otros,
ciertas introducciones hacia afuera.

Formas de fidelidades que ignoramos,
sólo en ellas es posible
postergar un poco la imposibilidad de todo.

We'll bury it all,
the arms, the motion, and the spade,
the passion of Fridays,
the banner of walking alone,
poverty—that debt—,
wealth—that other.

We'll bury it even with wisdom,
cutting the lumps of earth wisely,
or cutting them without noticing, wisely.

A relic of a glance
will stay on, floating like an absurd brush,
over the truce, kept both ways, with all that is absent.
And so much the better, then,
that there will be nobody to dig down deep
and discover that nothing is buried.

24 ⊢──────────────────────────────────

Lo enterraremos todo,
los brazos, el movimiento y la pala,
la pasión de los viernes,
la bandera de andar solos,
la pobreza, esa deuda,
la riqueza, esa otra.

Lo enterraremos hasta con sabiduría,
cortando sabiamente los terrones,
o cortándolos sin darnos cuenta, sabiamente.

Un resto de mirada
quedará flotando como un pincel absurdo
sobre la tregua doblemente fiel de todo ausente.
Y menos mal que no habrá nadie
para escarbar luego bien hondo
y descubrir que no hay nada enterrado.

On a night that should have been rain,
or on the wharf of a harbor that perhaps did not exist,
or on a clear afternoon, sitting at a table with no one,
a part of me fell off.
It didn't leave a hole.
More than that, it looked as though something had arrived
and not as though something had gone.
But now
on the nights without rain,
in the cities without wharves,
at the tables without afternoons,
suddenly I feel much more alone
and I can't even get up the courage to touch myself,
though everything seems to be in its place,
maybe even a little more so than before.
And I suspect that it might have been better
to stay in that part of me that was lost
instead of in this almost all
that has not fallen yet.

—|25

En una noche que debió ser lluvia
o en el muelle de un puerto tal vez inexistente
o en una tarde clara, sentado a una mesa sin nadie,
se me cayó una parte mía.
No ha dejado ningún hueco.
Es más: pareciera algo que ha llegado
y no algo que se ha ido.
Pero ahora,
en las noches sin lluvia,
en las ciudades sin muelles,
en las mesas sin tardes,
me siento de repente mucho más solo
y no me animo a palparme,
aunque todo parezca estar en su sitio,
quizá todavía un poco más que antes.
Y sospecho que hubiera sido preferible
quedarme en aquella perdida parte mía
y no en este casi todo
que aún sigue sin caer.

A long tunnel is coming closer to my mouth
and it's lowering my voice,
this ring that never finishes closing.

I've looked in vain for a word
to use as a finger for the ring
that's much nearer now.

If this tunnel were long enough
it would come back from its end each time,
it would be the finger, itself.

Only when there's a finger will the ring close.

26

Un largo túnel se me acerca a la boca
y me baja la voz,
este anillo que no termina nunca de cerrarse.

He buscado en vano una palabra
que sirva como dedo del anillo,
ahora mucho más cerca.

Si este túnel fuese suficientemente largo,
si retornara cada vez de su extremo,
él mismo sería el dedo.

Sólo cuando haya dedo se cerrará el anillo.

Third
Vertical
Poetry

||||

[1965]

Forms are born of an open hand.
But there is one that is born of the closed hand,
of the most intimate concentration of the hand,
of the closed hand that is not and will not become a fist.
Man is embodied around it
like the last fiber of the night
engendering the light that coincides with the night.

With this form
perhaps the conquest of zero would be possible,
the radiation of the point with no remainder,
the myth of the void in the word.

————————————————————————————————— ⊣ 1

Las formas nacen de la mano abierta.
Pero hay una que nace de la mano cerrada,
de la más íntima concentración de la mano,
de la mano cerrada que no es ni será puño.
El hombre se corporiza en torno a ella
como la fibra última de la noche
al engendrar la luz que coincide con la noche.

Quizá con esa forma sea posible
la conquista del cero,
la irradiación del punto sin residuo,
el mito de la nada en la palabra.

The other who bears my name
has begun to unknow me.
He wakes when I sleep,
he duplicates my persuasion of being absent,
he occupies my place as though the other were I,
he copies me in the showcases I do not love,
he sharpens my disused sockets,
renders idle the signs that join us,
and without me he visits the other versions of the night.

Following his example
now I am beginning to unknow myself.
It may be the only way to start
knowing ourselves.

2

El otro que lleva mi nombre
ha comenzado a desconocerme.
Se despierta donde yo me duermo,
me duplica la persuasión de estar ausente,
ocupa mi lugar como si el otro fuera yo,
me copia en las vidrieras que no amo,
me agudiza las cuencas desistidas,
descoloca los signos que nos unen
y visita sin mí las otras versiones de la noche.

Imitando su ejemplo,
ahora empiezo yo a desconocerme.
Tal vez no exista otra manera
de comenzar a conocernos.

There are footprints that do not coincide with their foot.
There are footsteps that anticipate their foot.
There are footsteps that make their foot.
There are footsteps that are more foot than the foot.

What can a foot do
when these things occur to it?
Nothing but
turn around toward the air.

———————————————————————————————————— ⊣3

Hay huellas que no coinciden con su pie.
Hay huellas que se anticipan a su pie.
Hay huellas que fabrican su pie.
Hay huellas que son más pie que el pie.

¿Qué puede hacer un pie
cuando le ocurren estas cosas?
Solamente
darse vuelta hacia el aire.

Life is a necessary precaution
like the shadow for the tree.
But there's something excessive,
as though life were to dodge its own leap
or the shadow throw itself backward and not forward.

Nakedness existed before the body.
And at times the body remembers it.

4 ├──┤

La vida es una precaución necesaria,
como la sombra para el árbol.
Pero hay algo que sobra,
como si la vida debiera esquivar su propio salto
o la sombra echarse atrás y no adelante.

La desnudez es anterior al cuerpo.
Y el cuerpo algunas veces lo recuerda.

Labyrinth of the bitter and the sweet,
of the ripe seasons before the harvest,
of the mistaken expressions in the exact forges,
of the dead sweetnesses around the fruit,
of the depraved acids
the blockade the tactile strategems of the afternoon,
thick walls of a climate that should have been future,
more future than the weather of any future day.

Taste drives mad
like a thread of blood that misses its veins.

Even the central trunk falls outside of the forest.

———|5

Laberinto de lo amargo y lo dulce,
de los tiempos maduros antes de la cosecha,
de los gestos equívocos en las fraguas exactas,
de los dulzores muertos alrededor del fruto,
de los resabios ácidos
que bloquean las táctiles maniobras de la tarde,
paredones de un clima que debió ser futuro,
más futuro que el tiempo de cualquier día futuro.

El sabor enloquece
como un hilo de sangre no acierta sus venas.

Hasta el tronco central cae afuera del bosque.

Why do the leaves occupy the place of the leaves
and not the place that's left between them?
Why does your glance occupy the hollow that's in front of
        reason
and not the one behind it?
Why do you remember that the light dies
and on the other hand forget that the shadow also dies?
Why is the heart of the air refined
until the song turns into another void in the void?
Why are you not silent in the exact place
where dying is the rightful presence
suspended from the tree of living?
Why these marks where the body ends
and not another body and another body and another?
Why this curve of why and not the sign
of an infinite vertical with a point above it?

6 ⊢——⊣

¿Por qué las hojas ocupan el lugar de las hojas
y no el que queda entre las hojas?
¿Por qué tu mirada ocupa el hueco que está delante de la razón
y no el que está detrás?
¿Por qué recuerdas que la luz se muere
y en cambio olvidas que también muere la sombra?
¿Por qué se afina el corazón del aire
hasta que la canción se vuelve otro vacío en el vacío?
¿Por qué no callas en el sitio exacto
donde morir es la presencia justa
suspendida del árbol de vivirse?
¿Por qué estas rayas donde el cuerpo cesa
y no otro cuerpo y otro cuerpo y otro?
¿Por qué esta curva del por qué y no el signo
de una recta sin fin y un punto encima?

If a thing changes form
it changes taste at the same time,
not only its taste to others
but also its taste to itself,
the flavor proper to its mode,
the relish of its unpeopled gut.

And if in the procession or dissipation of forms
this thing should find its own,
should meet it again in the sealed cloud of its origin,
its taste would be the same as before,
but only outwardly,
never to itself again.

{7

Si una cosa cambia de forma
cambia a la par de sabor,
no sólo su sabor hacia los otros
sino también su sabor hacia sí misma,
el gusto propio de su modo,
el paladeo de su entraña sin nadie.

Y si en el desfile o derroche de las formas
esa cosa recupera la suya,
la reencuentra en la nube sellada de su origen,
su sabor será el mismo de antes,
pero sólo hacia afuera
y ya nunca más hacia sí misma.

Crack of imminence in the heart,
while the foot of hope
dances its blue dance,
in love with its own shadow.

There is an expectant hymn
that cannot begin
as long as the dance has not finished
its cultivation of time.

It is a hymn backward,
an inverted imminence,
the last thread to tie the fountain
before its flow carries it away.

There are songs that sing,
there are others that are silent,
the deepest of all go backward
from the first letter.

8 |———————————————————————————|

Grieta en el corazón de la inminencia,
mientras el pie de la esperanza
baila su tiempo azul,
enamorado de su propia sombra.

Hay un himno expectante
que no puede empezar
mientras la danza no termine
su cultivo del tiempo.

Es un himno hacia atrás,
una inminencia invertida,
la última hebra para enlazar la fuente
antes que su fluencia se la lleve.

Hay canciones que cantan.
Hay otra que están quietas.
Las más hondas retroceden
desde su primera letra.

Sometimes I play that I catch up with myself.
I run with what I was
and with what I will be,
on the race of what I am.

And sometimes I play that I pass myself.
Then maybe I run
in the race of what I'm not.

But there's still another race
in which I'll play that I'm overtaken
and that will be the real one.

———9

Alguna vez juego a alcanzarme.
Corro con el que fui
y con el que seré
la carrera del que soy.

Y alguna vez juego a pasarme.
Corro entonces quizá
la carrera del que no soy.

Pero hay todavía otra carrera
en la que jugaré a hacerme pasar.
Y ésa será la carrera verdadera.

A lamp lit
in the middle of the day,
a light lost in the light.

And the theory of light is broken:
it's the greater light that recedes
as though a tree were to fall away from its fruit.

10

Una lámpara encendida
en medio del día,
una luz perdida en la luz.

Y la teoría de la luz se rompe:
la mayor retrocede
como un árbol que cayera del fruto.

The black rivers
don't have any mouths.
They simply descend or diminish
into certain places that are not black.

Nor is it possible to navigate their water,
their almost water, their too-much-water,
which looks the more solid for flowing.
Nor can we tell whether its blackness
is a language or a silence,
a real color
or a dark screen where
the world consumes its fictions.

Maybe the black rivers do not rise
anywhere either.

———————————————————————————— 11

Los ríos negros
no desembocan en ninguna parte.
Sencillamente caen o se encogen
en ciertos sitios que no son ni negros.

No es posible tampoco navegar su agua,
su casi agua, su excesiva agua,
que más parece sólido que fluye.
Ni es posible saber si su negrura
en un lenguaje o un silencio,
un color verdadero
o una pantalla prieta.

Tal vez los ríos negros
tampoco nazcan en ninguna parte.

Thoughts fall like leaves,
rot like fruit without teeth,
at times give shade
and at others resemble the withered lip
of a naked branch.

There are bodies that crack space,
break it as they fill it,
wound it as bread wounds certain mouths.
And there are shadows that heal that space,
close up the wounds that their bodies made,
restoring those bodies
from somewhere more intimate.

Thoughts fall like leaves
and rot like fruit,
but have no roots
and do not move in the wind.

12

Los pensamientos caen como las hojas,
se pudren como el fruto sin dientes,
dan sombra algunas veces
y otras son algo así como el labio demacrado
de una rama desnuda.

Hay cuerpos que agrietan el espacio,
lo quiebran al llenarlo,
lo hieren como el pan a ciertas bocas.
Y hay sombras que curan ese espacio,
le cicatrizan las heridas que le hicieran sus cuerpos,
reponiendo esos cuerpos
desde un lugar más íntimo.

Los pensamientos caen como las hojas
y se pudren como el fruto,
pero no tienen raíces
ni se mueven al viento.

Thinner than bodies and their shadows,
they neither crack space nor heal it:
they are a tree of space,
planted, without roots, in the center.

Más delgados que los cuerpos y sus sombras,
no agrietan ni curan el espacio:
son un árbol de espacio,
plantado, sin raíz, en el centro.

Without meaning to I break off with my fingers
a little branch.
I touch the place of the break
and my fingers then light up:
the whole of the branch
has passed into my fingers.
And in them it will stay
even if something in its turn breaks them off from me
and the whole of my fingers
passes into something else.

13

Involuntariamente quiebro con los dedos
una pequeña rama.
Toco el lugar de la ruptura
y mis dedos entonces se iluminan:
lo entero de la rama
ha pasado a mis dedos.
Y en ellos quedará,
aunque algo a su vez me los quiebre
y lo entero de mis dedos
pase a otra cosa.

Fourth
Vertical
Poetry

||||

[1969]

Life draws a tree
and death draws another one.
Life draws a nest
and death copies it.
Life draws a bird
to live in the nest
and right away death
draws another bird.

A hand that draws nothing
wanders among the drawings
and at times moves one of them.
For example:
a bird of life
occupies death's nest
on the tree that life drew.

Other times
the hand that draws nothing
blots out one drawing of the series.
For example:

———————————————————————————————— ┤1

La vida dibuja un árbol
y la muerte dibuja otro.
La vida dibuja un nido
y la muerte lo copia.
La vida dibuja un pájaro
para que habite el nido
y la muerte de inmediato
dibuja otro pájaro.

Una mano que no dibuja nada
se pasea entre todos los dibujos
y cada tanto cambia uno de sitio.
Por ejemplo:
el pájaro de la vida
ocupa el nido de la muerte
sobre el árbol dibujado por la vida.

Otras veces
la mano que no dibuja nada
borra un dibujo de la serie.
Por ejemplo:

the tree of death
holds the nest of death
but there's no bird in it.

And other times
the hand that draws nothing
itself changes
into an extra image
in the shape of a bird,
in the shape of a tree,
in the shape of a nest.
And then, only then,
nothing's missing and nothing's left over.
For example:
two birds
occupy life's nest
in death's tree.

Or life's tree
holds two nests
with only one bird in them.

---

el árbol de la muerte
sostiene el nido de la muerte,
pero no lo ocupa ningún pájaro.

Y otras veces
la mano que no dibuja nada
se convierte a sí misma
en imagen sobrante,
con figura de pájaro,
con figura de árbol,
con figura de nido.
Y entonces, sólo entonces,
no falta ni sobra nada.
Por ejemplo:
dos pájaros
ocupan el nido de la vida
sobre el árbol de la muerte

O el árbol de la vida
sostiene dos nidos
en los que habita un solo pájaro.

Or a single bird
lives in the one nest
on the tree of life
and the tree of death.

O un pájaro único
habita un solo nido
sobre el árbol de la vida
y el árbol de la muerte.

A fly is walking head downward on the ceiling,
a man is walking head downward in the street,
and some god is walking head downward through nothing.

You're the only one who's not walking this afternoon,
unless pure absences can invent
another form of walking which we don't know:
walking head up.

We will explore the meeting of love and stone,
the voyage of the hand to its pain,
the beach of flags the blood dreams of,
the celebration of being a man when a man wakes
and falls into manhood,
the fable that turns into a child,
the woman who's needed so we can love what we love
and even what we don't love.

And we will explore besides the empty space that you left in your
     poem,
the empty space that you left in each word

2 ├───┤

Una mosca anda cabeza abajo por el techo,
un hombre anda cabeza abajo por la calle
y algún dios anda cabeza abajo por la nada.

Tan sólo tú no andas esta tarde,
a menos que las ausencias puras
inventen otra forma de andar que no sabemos:
andar cabeza arriba.

Exploraremos el encuentro del amor y la piedra,
el viaje de la mano a su duelo,
la playa de banderas con que sueña la sangre,
la fiesta de ser hombre cuando el hombre despierta
y se cae en el hombre,
la fábula que se convierte en niño,
la mujer necesaria para amar lo que amamos
y hasta lo que no amamos.
Y exploraremos también el espacio vacío que dejaste en tu poema,
el espacio vacío que dejaste en cada palabra

and even in your own tomb
to build the future.

There we will meet you
and together we will break into walking head up.

(To Paul Eluard)

---

y hasta en tu propria tumba
para alzar el futuro.

Allí te encontraremos
y juntos echaremos a andar cabeza arriba.

(A Paul Eluard)

Somewhere there's a man
who sweats thought.
On his skin are drawn
the moist contours of a finer skin,
the wake of a navigation without a vessel.

When that man thinks light, he shines,
when he thinks death, he becomes polished,
when he remembers somebody, he acquires his features,
when he falls into himself he becomes dark like a well.

In him the color of night thoughts is visible
and it's obvious that no thought is without
its night and its day.
And also that there are colors and thoughts
that are not born of day or of night
but only when oblivion grows a little bigger.

That man is porous, like an earth with more life in it,
and at times when he dreams, he looks like a fire:

3 ⊢───

En alguna parte hay un hombre
que transpira pensamiento.
Sobre su piel se dibujan
los contornos húmedos de una piel más fina,
la estela de una navegación sin nave.

Cuando ese hombre piensa luz, ilumina,
cuando piensa muerte, se alisa,
cuando recuerda a alguien, adquiere sus rasgos,
cuando cae en sí mismo, se oscurece como un pozo.

En él se ve el color de los pensamientos nocturnos
y se aprende que ningún pensamiento carece
de su noche y su día.
Y también que hay colores y pensamientos
que no nacen de día ni de noche,
sino tan sólo cuando crece un poco más el olvido.

Ese hombre tiene la porosidad de una tierra más viva
y a veces, cuando sueña, toma aspecto de fuego,

splashes of a flame that feeds itself with flame,
writhings of calcined woods.

In that man love can be seen,
but only by someone who meets him and loves him.
And also in his flesh one could see god,
but only when one had stopped seeing all the rest.

(To Octavio Paz)

---

salpicaduras de una llama que se alimenta con llama,
retorcimientos de bosque calcinado.

A ese hombre se le puede ver el amor,
pero eso tan sólo quien lo encuentre y lo ame.
Y también se podría ver en su carne a dios,
pero sólo después de dejar de ver todo el resto.

(A Octavio Paz)

I'm awake.
I'm asleep.
I'm dreaming that I'm awake.
I'm dreaming that I'm asleep.
I'm dreaming that I'm dreaming.

I'm dreaming that I'm dreaming
that I'm awake.
I'm dreaming that I'm dreaming
that I'm asleep.
I'm dreaming that I'm dreaming
that I'm dreaming.

I'm awake.

4 ──────────────────────────────

Estoy despierto.
Me duermo.
Sueño que estoy despierto.
Sueño que me duermo.
Sueño que sueño.

Sueño que sueño
que estoy despierto.
Sueño que sueño
que me duermo.
Sueño que sueño
que sueño.

Estoy despierto.

A wall, a song,
and an air like the glaze on a ghost,
so that the song can rest on the wall.
On the other side, a man.
He didn't put up the wall
nor sing the song,
he's not even listening to it.
But the air glaze digs a circle in his shadow
with the song right in the middle.

The man's hunched down
(maybe he always was).
So the wall gets down
and climbs up his eyes.

A song
(never mind who's singing it),
a wall
(never mind who made it),

5

Un muro, una canción
y un aire como barniz de duende
para que la canción descanse sobre el muro.
Del otro lado, un hombre.
No ha levantado el muro
ni canta la canción,
ni siquiera la escucha.
Pero el aire barniz cava en su sombra un círculo
en donde la canción es justamente el centro.

El hombre está agachado
(tal vez lo estuvo siempre).
El muro baja entonces
y le sube los ojos.

Una canción
(no importa quien la cante),
un muro
(no importa quien lo ha hecho)

a smooth living air
(never mind where it's going).

If the man didn't exist
they'd have made him.

———————————————

y un aire liso y vivo
(no importa adonde vaya).

Si el hombre no existiera,
ellos lo habrían creado.

It's raining onto thought.

And thought is raining onto the world
like the remnants of a decimated net
whose cords can't manage to mesh.

It's raining inside thought.

And thought dams up and rains inside the world,
filling all the containers from the middle,
even the best watched and sealed.

It's raining under thought.

And thought's raining under the world,
wiping out the foundations of things
to build anew
the lodging of man and of life.

It's raining without thought.

———————————————————————————— 6

Llueve sobre el pensamiento.

Y el pensamiento llueve sobre el mundo
como los restos de una diezmada red
cuyas mallas no aciertan a encontrarse.

Llueve adentro del pensamiento.

Y el pensamiento rebalsa y llueve adentro del mundo,
colmando desde el centro todos los recipientes,
hasta los más guardados y sellados.

Llueve bajo el pensamiento.

Y el pensamiento llueve bajo el mundo,
borrando los cimientos de las cosas,
para fundar de nuevo
la habitación del hombre y de la vida.

Llueve sin el pensamiento.

And thought
goes on raining even without the world,
goes on raining even without the rain,
goes on raining.

Y el pensamiento
sigue lloviendo aun sin el mundo,
sigue lloviendo sin la lluvia,
sigue lloviendo.

If we knew the point
where something is going to break,
where the thread of kisses will be cut,
where a look will no longer meet another,
where the heart will leap toward another place,
we could put another point on that point
or at least go with it to its breaking.

If we knew the point
where something is going to melt into something,
where the desert will meet the rain,
where the embrace will touch life itself,
where my death will come closer to yours,
we could unwind that point like a streamer,
or at least sing it till we died.

If we knew the point
where something will always be something,
where the bone will not forget the flesh,

———————————————————————————————— 7

Si conociéramos el punto
donde va a romperse algo,
donde se cortará el hilo de los besos,
donde una mirada dejará de encontrarse con otra mirada,
donde el corazón saltará hacia otro sitio,
podríamos poner otro punto sobre ese punto
o por lo menos acompañarlo al romperse.

Si conociéramos el punto
donde algo va a fundirse con algo,
donde el desierto se encontrará con la lluvia,
donde el abrazo se tocará con la vida,
donde mi muerte se aproximará a la tuya,
podríamos desenvolver ese punto como una serpentina
o por lo menos cantarlo hasta morirnos.

Si conociéramos el punto
donde algo será siempre ese algo,
donde el hueso no olvidará a la carne,

where the fountain is mother to another fountain,
where the past will never be past,
we could leave that point and erase all the others,
or at least keep it in a safer place.

   (to Laura)

donde la fuente es madre de otra fuente,
donde el pasado nunca será pasado,
podríamos dejar sólo ese punto y borrar todos los otros
o guardarlo por lo menos en un lugar más seguro.

   (A Laura)

Fifth
Vertical
Poetry

||||

[1974]

In the root of the word
several loves are playing,
but also a sombre color
like the flags of a lost battle.

To speak is to live another way
but also to die another way,
as though to live were to die,
to die were to live.

In the root of the word
every love goes beyond what it loves
but comes back with a flower
imprudently dark
and knows that it can go no farther.

That is why, after the word,
in its root a space opens
where there is neither passion nor sarcasm,
a space out of which the most human absence
that inhabits anyone
can grow freely.

———————————————————————————————————| 1

En la raíz de la palabra
juegan varios amores,
pero también un sombrío color
parecido a las banderas de una batalla perdida.

Hablar es vivir de otra manera,
pero también morir de otra manera,
como si vivir fuera morir,
como si morir fuera vivir.

En la raíz de la palabra
todo amor va más allá de lo que ama,
pero vuelve con una flor imprudentemente oscura
y reconoce que no puede ir más allá.

Es por eso que después de la palabra
en su raíz se abre un espacio sin pasión ni sarcasmo,
un espacio desde el cual puede crecer ya libremente
la ausencia más humana que habita en el hombre.

The emptiness of the day
condenses into a point
that falls like a drop
into the river.

The fullness of the day
condenses into a minute orifice
that sucks that drop
out of the river.

From what fullness to what emptiness
or from what emptiness to what fullness
is the river flowing?

———————————————————————————————————————|2

Lo vacío del día
se condensa en un punto
que cae como una gota
en el río.

Lo lleno del día
se condensa en un mínimo orificio
que aspira aquella gota
del río.

¿Desde qué lleno a qué vacío
o desde qué vacío a qué lleno
corre el río?

The eye draws on the white ceiling
a little black line.
The ceiling takes up the eye's illusion
and turns black.
Then the line erases itself
and the eye closes.

Thus solitude is born.

3 ⊢————————————————————————————

El ojo traza en el techo blanco
una pequeña raya negra.
El techo asume la ilusión del ojo
y se vuelve negro.
La raya se borra entonces
y el ojo se cierra.

Así nace la soledad.

Its own thirst sustains it.
The things all around it sustain it.
The desire to exist sustains it.
A glass made of water.

A glass made of water
and full of water.
The image from inside the mirror.
The end of flowing over and the falling.
A water with its own thirst for water.

4

Su propia transparencia lo sostiene.
El cerco de las cosas lo sostiene.
El deseo de que exista lo sostiene.
Un vaso hecho de agua.

Un vaso hecho de agua
y lleno de agua.
La imagen desde adentro del espejo.
El final del derrame y la caída.
Un agua con su sed propia de agua.

Each hand arranges its cloud
in a separate sky.

But one day it finds its cloud
in everyone's sky.

Only then can it become once more
the piece of promised land
that it was before it was a hand.

Only then will its cloud
rain upon it.

5 ├──┤

Cada mano coloca su nube
en un cielo distinto.

Pero un día la encuentra
en el cielo de todos.

Sólo entonces puede volver a ser
el pedazo de tierra prometida
que era antes de ser mano.

Sólo entonces su nube
lloverá sobre ella.

Each thing makes hands for itself.
The tree for example
to divide the wind.

Each thing makes feet for itself.
The house for example
to follow somebody.

Each thing makes eyes for itself.
The arrow for example
to hit the target.

Each thing makes a tongue for itself.
The glass for example
to talk with the wine.

Each thing makes a story for itself.
The water for example
to get clean away.

---- 6

Cada cosa se fabrica unas manos.
El árbol, por ejemplo,
para repartir el viento.

Cada cosa se fabrica unos pies.
La casa, por ejemplo,
para seguir al hombre.

Cada cosa se fabrica unos ojos.
La flecha, por ejemplo,
para entrar en el blanco.

Cada cosa se fabrica una lengua.
La copa, por ejemplo,
para hablar con el vino.

Cada cosa se fabrica una historia.
El agua, por ejemplo,
para huir más segura.

And man in the meantime
abandons his hands
abandons his feet
abandons his eyes
abandons his tongue
abandons his story
to make another man
and continue to lead
this unheard-of procession
this concentric otherness
whose center also abandons its own point
to make another center.

Y mientras tanto el hombre
abandona sus manos,
abandona sus pies,
abandona sus ojos,
abandona su lengua,
abandona su historia,
para fabricar otro hombre
y continuar a la vanguardia
de esta inaudita procesión,
de esta otredad concéntrica,
cuyo centro también abandona su punto
para fabricar otro centro.

The faces that you've discarded
have remained under your face
and sometimes they bulge out
as though your skin could not contain them all.

The hands that you've discarded
swell up sometimes in your hand
and absorb things or release them
like growing sponges.

The lives that you've abandoned
survive you in your own shadow
and one day they will storm you like a life
to die perhaps all at once.

———————————————————————————————| 7

Los rostros que has ido abandonando
se han quedado debajo de tu rostro
y a veces te sobresalen
como si tu piel no alcanzara para todos.

Las manos que has ido abandonando
te abultan a veces en la mano
y te absorben las cosas o las sueltan
como esponjas crecientes.

Las vidas que has ido abandonando
te sobreviven en tu propia sombra
y algún día te asaltarán como una vida,
tal vez para morir una vez sola.

The creatures of afternoon
light the bonfires of their imagination
and hold up the sky
with the gossamer wires of the waning light.

The creatures of afternoon
know that they should not speak
for speech is an atavism
from other ages of the day.

Even though their words perhaps
might sustain the night.

8 ⊢───

Las criaturas de la tarde
encienden las fogatas de su imaginación
y sostienen el cielo
con los finísmos alambres de la luz que se va.

Las criaturas de la tarde
saben que no deben hablar,
porque hablar es un atavismo
de otras edades del día.

Aunque sus palabras
podrían tal vez sostener a la noche.

A glass of water
assembles another afternoon
inside the afternoon,
a separate conglomeration of time.
And for a moment the door of perception opens,
the door that does not have to be pushed
to close.

And I drink that glass
of water twice.

——————————————————————————————————| 9

Un vaso de agua
organiza otra tarde adentro de la tarde,
un conglomerado de tiempo distinto.
Y se abre por un momento la puerta del sentido,
la puerta que no es preciso empujar
para que se cierre.

Y yo bebo dos veces
ese vaso de agua.

Embrace your head
as though you could shelter it.

Embrace it until thought
can embrace thought.

Embrace it until you feel
the thought of your arms.

10 ─────────────────────────────────

Abrazarse la cabeza
como si se le pudiera dar un refugio.

Abrazarla hasta que el pensamiento
pueda abrazar al pensamiento.

Abrazarla hasta sentir
el pensamiento en los brazos.

Sixth

Vertical

Poetry

||||

[1976]

My sight is waiting for me in things
to look out of them at me
and take my sight away from me.

My memory is waiting for me in things
to show me that forgetting does not exist.

And things depend on me
as though I who have no root
were the root they do not have.

Can it be that things
are waiting in me too?

Can it be that all that exists
is waiting outside itself?

Can it be that my arms at the end
will be open to embrace me?

—— 1

Mi mirada me espera en las cosas,
para mirarme desde ellas
y despojarme de mi mirada.

Mi memoria me espera en las cosas
para demostrarme que no existe el olvido.

Y las cosas se apoyan en mí,
como si yo, que no tengo raíz,
fuera la raíz que les falta.

¿Es que tal vez las cosas
también se esperan en mí?

¿Es que todo lo que existe
se está esperando afuera de sí mismo?

¿Es que al final estarán mis brazos
abiertos para abrazarme?

It is easy to imitate at the beginning the voice of the end
to make a mirror look like water
or draw the outline of solitude carefully on cardboard.

But to live is to return to wandering towers
floating trees
colleges of clouds
assemblies of omens
and sudden duplicities of anguish
that shake us like coughing or hiccoughs or spasms from the
      void.

The breast the eyes and other things that close
learn their calling in us
until the climate is completed
and death seals the apprenticeship.

One must cry out in the desert
before one can people the desert.

2 ├───────────────────────────────────

Es fácil imitar al comienzo la voz del final,
simular el agua con un vidrio
o recortar cuidadosamente la soledad sobre un cartón.

Pero vivir es frecuentar torres nómades,
árboles flotantes,
colegios de nubes,
convocatorias de presagios
y repentinas duplicidades de la angustia
que nos sacuden como tos o hipo o espasmos del abismo.

El pecho, los ojos y otras cosas que se cierran
aprenden en nosotros su oficio,
hasta que el clima se completa
y la muerte clausura el aprendizaje.

Es necesario gritar en el desierto,
antes de poder poblar el desierto.

There are few complete deaths.
The cemeteries are full of frauds.
The streets are full of ghosts.

There are few complete deaths.
But the bird knows on which branch to perch last
and the tree knows where the bird ends.

There are few complete deaths.
Each time death is more uncertain.
Death is something that life is trying out
and sometimes it takes two lives
to be able to complete one death.

There are few complete deaths.
The bells toll the same thing always,
but reality offers no guarantees
and it takes more than just living to die.

---|3

Hay pocas muertes enteras.
Los cementerios están llenos de fraudes.
Las calles están llenas de fantasmas.

Hay pocas muertes enteras.
Pero el pájaro sabe en qué rama última se posa
y el árbol sabe dónde termina el pájaro.

Hay pocas muertes enteras.
La muerte es cada vez más insegura.
La muerte es una experiencia de la vida.
Y a veces se necesitan dos vidas
para poder completar una muerte.

Hay pocas muertes enteras.
Las campanas doblan siempre lo mismo.
Pero la realidad ya no ofrece garantías
y no basta vivir para morir.

The bell is full of wind
though it does not ring.
The bird is full of flight
though it is still.
The sky is full of clouds
though it is alone.
The word is full of voice
though no one speaks it.
Everything is full of fleeing
though there are no roads.

Everything is fleeing
toward its presence.

4 ├────────────────────────────────

La campana está llena de viento,
aunque no suene.
El pájaro está lleno de vuelo,
aunque esté quieto.
El cielo está lleno de nubes,
aunque esté solo.
La palabra está llena de voz,
aunque nadie la diga.
Toda cosa está llena de fugas,
aunque no haya caminos.

Todas las cosas huyen
hacia su presencia.

The lightning flash of beauty
creates the eternity in back of the eye.

The lightning flash of love
creates the eternity in back of oblivion.

The lightning flash of life
creates the eternity in the other face of death.

The lightning flash of the moment
creates the eternity on the other side of time.

All light illumines.
It may even dazzle.
But clarity is on the other side of the light.

———————————————————————————————|5

El relámpago de la belleza
crea la eternidad en el revés del ojo.

El relámpago del amor
crea la eternidad en la espalda del olvido.

El relámpago de la vida
crea la eternidad en la otra cara de la muerte.

El relámpago del instante
crea la eternidad del otro lado del tiempo.

Toda luz ilumina.
Y hasta quizá deslumbra.
Pero la claridad está en el reverso de la luz.

Where does it go
this vine that climbs the air?

There are limits even up there.

And besides, the air
is climbing the vine.

6 ⊢————————————————————————————⊣

¿Hasta dónde podrá subir
la enredadera que se apoya en el aire?

También arriba hay límites.

Y también el aire
se apoya en la enredadera.

Solitude calls me by every name
except mine.

Solitude even calls me sometimes by your name.

But other times
solitude calls me by its own name.

Maybe one day
I will be able to call solitude by my name
and then surely
it will have to answer me.

—————————————————————————————— 7

La soledad me llama con todos los nombres,
menos con el mío.

Las soledad me llama también a veces con tu nombre.

Pero hay otras veces
en que la soledad me llama con su propio nombre.

Quizás algún día
pueda yo llamar a la soledad con mi nombre.
Y entonces, seguramente,
habrá de responderme.

There is a door that's open
but we have to break in, just the same.

We don't know what's behind it
but the calling is coming from in there.

We could go somewhere else
but we've come from somewhere else.

We're outside and we know it
but maybe everything is outside.

This is the door we keep looking for
but it's supposed to be closed.

Here we can't get past what's open.
How can you pass what doesn't exist?

We may have to shut the only door
in order to get in.

8 |————————————————————————————————————|

Hay una puerta abierta
y sin embargo hay que forzarla.

No conocemos qué hay detrás,
pero de allí surge el llamado.

Podemos ir hacia otra parte,
pero venimos de otra parte.

Estamos fuera y lo sabemos
pero quizá todo es afuera.

Siempre buscamos esta puerta,
pero debiera estar cerrada.

Aquí lo abierto es lo infranqueable.
¿Cómo pasar lo que no existe?

Hay que cerrar la única puerta
para poder tal vez entrar.

Seventh

Vertical

Poetry

||||

[1982]

Use your own hand for a pillow.
The sky uses it clouds,
the earth its clods,
and the falling tree
its own leaves.

That is the only way
to hear the song without distance,
the song that does not enter the ear
because it is in the ear,
the only song that is never repeated.

Everyone needs one
untranslatable song.

———————————————————————————————— ⊣1

Usar la propia mano como almohada.
El cielo lo hace con sus nubes,
la tierra con sus terrones
y el árbol que cae
con su propio follaje.

Sólo así puede escucharse
la canción sin distancia,
la canción que no entra en el oído
porque está en el oído,
la única canción que no se repite.

Todo hombre necesita
una canción intraducible.

To transplant the memories
of one man into other men
as a rootstock is transplanted
from one piece of ground to another.
Maybe that way you could start
another kind of greeting and recognition
instead of these ridiculous faces we make
that thin the air.

And if someone could transplant his memories
outside of human kind
or graft them onto a tree or a rock
or perhaps onto the relative silence
that lies in wait between particular columns
maybe they could begin a new way of feeling
instead of these shipwrecked dodges
with which we explain nothing
not even absence.

2 ⊢───

Trasplantar los recuerdos
de un hombre a otros hombres,
como se trasplanta una cepa
de un terreno a otro terreno.
Tal vez así podría iniciarse
otra forma del saludo y el reconocimiento,
para reemplazar estos gestos absurdos
que enrarecen el aire.

Y si el hombre pudiera trasplantar sus recuerdos
afuera de los hombres
o injertarlos en un árbol o una roca
o quizá en el relativo silencio
que aguarda entre ciertas columnas,
tal vez podría comenzar otra forma del sentido,
en lugar de estas pobres maniobras de náufragos
con las que no explicamos nada,
ni siquiera la ausencia.

If a man could transplant his memories
death would not exist
and neither dreams nor madness
would be necessary.
Even love would not be necessary.

Si pudiera el hombre trasplantar sus recuerdos,
no existiría la muerte.
Y ya no serían necesarios tampoco
el sueño y la locura.
No sería necesario ni siquiera el amor.

We have a sign on the forehead
and another on the back of the neck.
Sometimes it appears to us
that forward is the sign of life
and backward that of death.
But some days it is the other way around.
And in other days still
we have the same sign
facing forward and backward.

In any case
this game proves to us
that we exist between two signs
or at least inside of one.

Yet there is
still another possibility:
that it's all about
no sign at all
from two points of view.

3 |————————————————————————————————

Llevamos una señal en la frente
y otra señal en la nuca.
A veces nos parece
que adelante está el signo de la vida
y atrás el de la muerte.
Pero hay días en que el orden se invierte.
Y hay todavía otros días
en que llevamos adelante y atrás
la misma señal.

De cualquier modo,
este juego nos prueba
que existimos entre dos señales
o por lo menos dentro de una.

Sin embargo,
queda aún otra posibilidad:
que se trate de ninguna señal
y dos puntos de vista.

From under everything
wells the voice of a bell.
It's not to summon to a temple
nor announce spring
nor accompany a corpse.
It's only to ring
as a man would
with open eyes
if he were a bell.
It's only to net lost birds
in a louder air.
It's only
so that the song can go on
without going anywhere.

A simple bell
that rings from down there
like a natural motion
with no one moving it

4

Desde abajo de todo
brota la voz de una campana.
No sirve para llamar al templo,
ni para anunciar la primavera,
ni para acompañar a un muerto.
Sólo sirve para sonar
como lo haría un hombre
con los ojos abiertos
si fuera una campana.
Sólo sirve
para rodear a los pájaros perdidos
con un aire más sonoro.
Sólo sirve
para que dure el canto
que no va a ninguna parte.

Una simple campana
que suena desde abajo
como un movimiento natural,
sin que nadie la agite,

no one hearing it
as though under everything
there were nothing but
the disinterested ringing of a bell.

sin que nadie la oiga,
como si el fondo de todo
no fuera otra cosa
que el desinteresado tañer de una campana.

My walk, my insanity, my passion in the night
assume only
that today I'm more alive
and tomorrow more dead.

That's why I don't go adoring curtains
nor correcting ghost stories
nor exchanging coins for insomnias
nor beating the moon with sticks
nor covering hysteria with paragraphs
nor kissing the back of my hand
to prove that I believe.

My presence in the night
grows like a tapestry that someone is watching.
In the night I learned the silence of being.
The silence of not being is not learned
but both have their names in the night.

———————————————————————————————— 5

Mi andanza, mi locura, mi pasión en la noche
no tienen más supuestos
que el estar hoy más vivo
y mañana más muerto.

Por eso no ando incensando velos,
ni corrigiendo historias de fantasmas,
ni intercambiando insomnios por monedas,
ni pegándole palos a la luna,
ni cubriendo de párrafos la histeria,
ni besándome el dorso de la mano
para probar mi fe en alguna cosa.

Mi presencia en la noche
crece como un tapiz que alguien contempla.
Yo he aprendido en la noche el silencio de ser.
El silencio de no ser no se aprende.
Pero los dos se nombran en la noche.

Trim away the space between things
so that it no longer runs over onto them,
and so resist the imperialism of space
and its cruel preference for the void.

Everything is in danger.
Everything can be wiped out.
But space also is in danger.
It may not exist.

6 ├─────────────────────────────────────

Recortar el espacio que queda entre las cosas
para que no desborde sobre ellas,
para contrarrestar el imperialismo del espacio
y su cruel inclinación hacia el vacío.

Toda cosa peligra.
Toda cosa puede ser borrada.
Pero también el espacio peligra:
podría no existir el espacio.

Each thing is a river
in another river
and there may be another.

But these rivers
never flow
in the same direction
which is why we do not know
where the sea is.

And they do not flow
at the same speed either
which is why we do not know
where the shore is,
the shore where somebody
can at least stand
to salvage something
from all that the dark
currents of the rivers
in the rivers
are dragging away.

⊣7

Cada cosa es un río
adentro de otro río
y quizás otro.

Pero esos ríos
no se deslizan nunca
en el mismo sentido.
Por eso no sabemos
adónde queda el mar.

Y no corren tampoco
con la misma rapidez.
Por eso ni sabemos
adónde está la orilla,
la orilla en la que al menos
alguien podría pararse
para rescatar algo de lo mucho que arrastran
las corrientes oscuras
de los ríos adentro de los ríos.

These rivers that do not
even flow with beds under them
and a mantle of air over them,
because those too
long ago became part of the rivers.

Or maybe it's the other way around:
the river bed is above
and the air underneath.

So that someone might imagine
a glimpse of a watch tower
in the boundless and unpausing flow.

Esos ríos que ni siquiera corren
con un lecho debajo
y una capa de aire arriba,
porque también ellos
suelen estar adentro de los ríos.

O tal vez al revés:
quizá esté el lecho arriba
y el aire en cambio abajo.

Por si alguien creyera vislumbrar una atalaya
en el derrame sin límite y sin pausa.

Just as we cannot
keep the glance steady for long
so we cannot keep up happiness for long
nor take the winding down of love
the free gift of thought
the earth suspended in its canticle.

We cannot even stand for long
the proportions of silence
when something visits it,
still less
when nothing visits it.

Man cannot stand man much of the time
nor what is not man

and yet he can hold up
the limitless weight
of all that does not exist.

———|8

Así como no podemos
sostener mucho tiempo una mirada,
tampoco podemos sostener mucho tiempo la alegría,
la espiral del amor,
la gratuidad del pensamiento,
la tierra en suspensión del cántico.

No podemos ni siquiera sostener mucho tiempo
las proporciones del silencio
cuando algo lo visita.
Y menos todavía
cuando nada lo visita.

El hombre no puede sostener mucho tiempo al hombre,
ni tampoco a lo que no es el hombre.

Y sin embargo puede
soportar el peso inexorable
de lo que no existe.

Each half of the world
holds up the other
but what holds up the two halves?

There is still beauty.
There is still life.
And the human heart
tells over the beads of the rosary
in strokes of eternity
and lapses of time
respecting the absent links
and the chain that is left over.

9 ⊢──────────────────────────────

Cada mitad del mundo
sostiene a la otra,
pero qué sostiene a las dos mitades.

La belleza todavía existe.
La vida todavía existe.
Y el corazón del hombre
pasa las cuentas del rosario
con que a golpes de eternidad
y descansos de tiempo
enumera los eslabones que faltan
y la cadena que sobra.

The heart moulds summits,
a potter of heights,
but sometimes those heights themselves
keep it up there.

A prisoner then of its own making
it grows thin at the point
that it cannot pass through again
and weeps drop by drop
over lost time.

There are lives that are like rain.
Rain is also the testimony
of hearts imprisoned high up.

———————————————————————————— ⊣10

El corazón modela cimas,
alfarero de alturas,
pero a veces esas mismas alturas
le impiden descender.

Prisionero entonces de su propio trabajo,
se adelgaza en el límite del cegado retorno
y llueve gota a gota
sobre el tiempo perdido.

Hay vidas que son como la lluvia.
La lluvia es también el testimonio
de corazones cautivos más arriba.

In the gut of summer
like a clear thread
echoes the voice of the ice cream seller.

It is not childhood coming back.
It is not something divine dressed in white.
It is not the moon in the daytime.

It is only the possible
showing us that it exists.

The impossible never raises its voice.

11 |————————————————————————————————————|

En las entrañas del verano,
como una fibra más clara,
repercute la voz del heladero.

No es la infancia que vuelve.
No es algo de dios que se ha vestido de blanco.
No es una luna en el día.

Es sólo lo posible
que nos demuestra su existencia.

Lo imposible no levanta nunca la voz.

The prompting of my shadow
has taught me to be humble.
It doesn't care whether it draws me
on the bony seats of the trains
early in the morning,
on the seamless walls of the cemeteries
or on the penumbras of short cuts
that betray the city.

The frame doesn't matter to it,
not the stilted epigraphs.
My shadow impersonates me step by step,
misleads me into the sockets of all the corners,
never answers my questions.

My shadow has taught me to adopt other shadows.

My shadow has put me in my place.

———|12

La iniciativa de mi sombra
me ha enseñado a ser humilde.
Ella me dibuja indiferentemente
sobre los demarcados asientos
de los trenes de la madrugada,
sobre los muros sin costura de los cementerios
o sobre la penumbra de los atajos
que traicionan a la ciudad.

El marco no interesa,
como tampoco los tullidos epígrafes.
Mi sombra me desmiente a cada paso,
me despista en el hueco de todas las esquinas
y no contesta a mis preguntas.

Mi sombra me ha enseñado a adoptar otras sombras.

Mi sombra me ha colocado en mi justo lugar.

The advantage of the flat men
is that they can live in flat houses
and think flat thoughts
that fit into the pages of books.

They don't need steps in the night
nor branches in the trees.
They don't need many rooms
nor temples nor caresses nor locks.

The flat men stop up their sight
with corks.
Death cannot get into their houses.
No room.

The flat men always mislead us
though they have no shadows.
The moon weaves hearts for them
and time weaves results for them.

13 ┝————————————————————————————————

La ventaja de los hombres planos
es que pueden vivir en casas planas
y pensar pensamientos planos,
que caben entre las hojas de los libros.

No necesitan pasos en la noche
ni ramas en los árboles.
No necesitan muchas habitaciones,
ni templos, ni caricias, ni candados.

Los hombres planos tapan las miradas
con tapones de corcho.
Y en sus casas no puede entrar la muerte
porque no encuentra espacio.

Los hombres planos siempre nos despistan,
aunque no tengan sombra.
La luna les va tejiendo corazones
y el tiempo les va tejiendo resultados.

If they need a lamp there's always some candle lit.
If they need a voice the wind speaks for them.
All they need is an outline to be there
as their nights arrive without contours.

Si les falta un candil, siempre arde alguna vela.
Si les falta la voz, el viento los disfraza.
Y les basta un perfil para ubicarse,
mientras llega su noche sin relieves.

The shadow erases the tracks of its body
but the body cannot
erase the tracks of its shadow.

The shadow outlasts the body.
It might be good to give it
some of our dream to keep.
Or send it ahead toward death
to wipe out death's tracks too.

For death is a body and not a shadow.
A body with no shadow.

14 ⊢───────────────────────────────────

La sombra borra las huellas de su cuerpo,
pero el cuerpo no puede
borrar las huellas de su sombra.

La sombra dura más que su cuerpo.
Tal vez convendría entonces descargar en ella
parte de nuestro sueño.
O quizá anticiparla hacia la muerte,
por si puede también borrar sus huellas.

Porque la muerte es un cuerpo y no una sombra.
Un cuerpo sin sombra.

Every time that I go into the night
I feel that my entry is plural,
not simply because all of my characters are present
but because all of the parts of the night
take me in.

But every time I come out of the night
I feel that I come out as one,
not just because all of my characters have melted together
but because all of the parts of the night as well
have become one.

So if I have to go into the night through some doorway
on the other hand I am able to come out through the eye of a
        needle.
Now I have to learn to go in
through the eye of a needle.

—————————————————————————————————|15

Cada vez que entro en la noche
siento que mi ingreso es plural,
no sólo porque acuden todos mis personajes,
sino porque además me reciben
todas las partes de la noche.

Pero cada vez que emerjo de la noche
siento que mi salida es unitaria,
no sólo porque todos mis personajes se han fundido en uno,
sino porque además todas las partes de la noche
se han vuelto una sola.

Por eso, si bien debo entrar en la noche por alguna puerta,
puedo un cambio salir por el ojo de una aguja.
Ahora debo aprender a entrar
por el ojo de una aguja.

Things imitate us.
A paper caught by the wind
acts like a stumbling human.
Noises learn to talk like us.
Clothes take on our shapes.

Things imitate us
but we will end up
imitating them.

16 |————————————————————————————

Las cosas nos imitan.
Un papel arrastrado por el viento
reproduce los tropezones del hombre.
Los ruidos aprenden a hablar como nosotros.
La ropa adquiere nuestra forma.

Las cosas nos imitan.
Pero al final
nosotros imitaremos a las cosas.

Every silence is a magic space
with a hidden rite,
the womb of a summoning word,
and an essential detail of antisilence.

The hidden rite may be for example
a death in winter.
The word in the womb
may be simply the word "forget."
And the detail of antisilence
may be the sound of a few clods striking the earth.

Or the rite the rocking of a tenderness in the night,
the word a proper name drowning,
and the indispensable detail of antisilence
a little water flowing through the dream of the world.

Or the rite may be the solitude of a poem,
the word the sign that every poem hides,

———————————————————————— 17

Todo silencio es un espacio mágico,
con un rito escondido,
la matriz de una palabra convocatoria
y un imprescindible detalle de antisilencio.

El rito escondido puede ser por ejemplo
una muerte en invierno,
la palabra en gestación
puede ser sencillamente la palabra olvido
y el detalle de antisilencio
puede ser el golpe de unos terrones contra la tierra.

O el rito la oscilación de una ternura en la noche,
la palabra, un nombre propio que se ahoga,
y el infaltable detalle de antisilencio
un poco de agua que se desliza por el sueño del mundo.

O el rito puede ser la soledad de un poema,
la palabra el signo que todo poema oculta,

and the point of antisilence
the sound of the hand calling from inside the poem.

Silence is a temple
that needs no god.

---

y el punto de antisilencio
el sonido de la mano que llama desde adentro del poema.

El silencio es un templo
que no necesita dios.

Invent a return of the world
after its disappearance.
And invent a return to that world
after our disappearance.
And unite the two memories
to join up all the details.

It must be tested endlessly
to see whether it holds up.

—————————————————————————————| 18

Inventar el regreso del mundo
después de su desaparición.
E inventar un regreso a ese mundo
desde nuestra desaparición.
Y reunir las dos memorias,
para juntar todos los detalles.

Hay que ponerle pruebas al infinito,
para ver si resiste.

Eighth

Vertical

Poetry

||||

[1984]

From time to time we must begin to do without writing
and learn to live with the white page,
with its too smooth flatness
and its too open horizon.

We must leave our images in mid-air
to get closer to our transfigurations
and converse with them at the edge of the whiteness
with no letter for witness.

Hay que empezar a abandonar cada tanto la escritura
y aprender a convivir con la página en blanco,
con su llanura demasiado lisa,
con su horizonte demasiado abierto.

Hay que dejar en suspenso nuestras figuraciones
para aproximarnos a nuestras transfiguraciones
y dialogar con ellas en el extremo del blanco,
sin tener siquiera la letra como testigo.

Ninth

Vertical

Poetry

||||

[1988]

To die, but far away.
Not here
where everything is a perverse
conspiracy of life,
even the other dead.

To die far away.
Not here
where death by now is a betrayal,
a greater betrayal than anywhere else.

To die far away.
Not here
where solitude rests now and then
like an animal stretched out
forgetting its spur of madness.

To die far away.
Not here
where everyone always

———————————————————————————————————|1

Morir, pero lejos.
No aquí,
donde todo es una aviesa
conspiración de la vida,
hasta las otras muertes.

Morir lejos.
No aquí,
donde morir es ya una traición,
más traición que en otra parte.

Morir lejos.
No aquí,
donde la soledad descansa a ratos
como si fuera un animal tendido,
olvidando su espuela de locura.

Morir lejos.
No aquí,
donde cada uno se duerme

goes to sleep in the same place
yet always wakes up somewhere else.

To die far away.
Not here.
To die where nobody is waiting for us
and there may be a place to die.

---

siempre en el mismo sitio,
aunque despierte siempre en otro.

Morir lejos.
No aquí.
Morir donde nadie nos espere,
donde haya lugar para morir.

The roads leading upward
never get there.
The roads leading downward
always get there.

Then there are the roads in between.

But sooner or later every road
leads up or down.

——————————————————————————————| 2

Los caminos hacia arriba
nunca llegan.
Los caminos hacia abajo
siempre llegan.

Hay también caminos intermedios.

Pero antes o después todo camino
va hacia arriba o abajo.

Interior deserts,
vague litanies for someone who died
leaving all the doors open.
A gray cloak over another cloak of no color.
Excessive densities.
Even the wind casts a shadow.
Mockery of the landscape.

Nothing left to call to
but a flat dark sun
or an endless rain.
Or wipe out the landscape
with the wind and its shadow.

And there is one further resort:
drive the desert mad
until it turns into water
and drinks itself.

It is better to madden the desert
than to live there.

3 |————————————————————————————

Desiertos interiores,
vagos responsos por un muerto
que dejó todas las puertas abiertas.
Una capa gris sobre otra sin color.
Densidades excesivas.
Hasta el viento hace sombra.
Irrisión del paisaje.

Sólo queda apelar
a un plano sol oscuro
o a una lluvia para siempre
o borrar el paisaje
con el viento y su sombra.

Y también queda el recurso
de enloquecer al desierto,
para que se convierta en agua
y se beba a sí mismo.

Enloquecer al desierto
es mejor que poblarlo.

You can put out all the fires
but never put an end to the smoke.

The one who did not rise to the dignity of fire
ends by conforming to the modesty of smoke.
The one who did not have a hand in lighting it
ends up by giving that hand
and being left alone with the smoke.
The one who does not pretend to warm anything
or even to being warmed
hides in the secret of being smoke.

But the secret of smoke is double.
First: the smoke warms too.
Second, and most important:
the smoke is older than the fire.

⊣4

Se podrá apagar todos los fuegos
pero nunca se acabará el humo.

Aquello que no alcanzó la dignidad del fuego
termina conformándose con la humildad del humo.
Aquello que no tuvo una mano que lo encendiera
termina por renunciar a esa mano
y se queda a solas con el humo.
Aquello que no pretende calentar nada,
ni siquiera calentarse,
se refugia en el secreto de ser humo.

Pero el secreto del humo es doble.
Primero: también el humo calienta.
Segundo y principal:
el humo es anterior al fuego.

A note has been lost.
We do not know the compass nor the scale,
but the work dissolves toward the west
like an arrow brushed by a feather as it passes.

A line has strayed.
We do not know the figure nor the picture
but the image is herded toward the margin
like a festival into whose center a black fruit falls.

A color has been wiped out.
We do not know in what zone or what world
but this irreparable almost nothing
is a wound in everything forever.

5 |————————————————————————————|

Se ha perdido una nota.
No sabemos el compás ni la escala,
pero la obra se descompone hacia el poniente
como una flecha rozada al pasar por una pluma.

Se ha extraviado una línea.
No sabemos la figura o el cuadro,
pero la imagen se acorrala contra un borde
como una fiesta en cuyo centro cae un fruto negro.

Se ha borrado un matiz.
No sabemos en qué zona o qué mundo,
pero ese casi nada irreparable
lo hiere todo para siempre.

A
Recent
Poem

||||

For one moment
the eyes of the living
met the eyes of the dead.
And they did not strike like fists
nor dent the edge of contact
nor was there any eyelid or eclipse
to restrict the dangerous glance between them.

The eyes of the living and the dead
met only for a moment
to excavate at the place of their meeting
a lap less rough,
a space without danger,
a zone along the line between life and death.

Por un instante se encontraron
las miradas de los vivos
y las miradas de los muertos.
Y no chocaron como puños,
ni mellaron el filo del contacto,
ni hubo tampoco ningún párpado o eclipse
que censurara la peligrosa entrevisión.

Las miradas de los vivos y los muertos
se encontraron nada más que un instante
para excavar en el sitio del encuentro
un regazo menos áspero,
un espacio no comprometido,
una zona al margen de la vida y la muerte.

Design by David Bullen
Typeset in Mergenthaler Electra
by Wilsted & Taylor
with Deepdene display
Printed by Malloy Lithographing
on acid-free paper